CHRISTIAN POEMS

HONOURING CHRIST

S. K. Haddad

Kingdom Publishers

Christian Poems
Honouring Christ
Copyright© S. K. Haddad

All rights reserved. No part of this book may be reproduced in any form by photocopying or any electronic or mechanical means, including information storage or retrieval systems, without permission in writing from both the copyright owner and the publisher of the book. The right of S. K. Haddad to be identified as the author of this work has been asserted by him in accordance with the Copyright, Designs and Patents Act 1988 and any subsequent amendments thereto.
A catalogue record for this book is available from the British Library.

All Scripture Quotations have been taken from the King James Version of the Bible.

ISBN: 978-1-911697-16-9

1st Edition by Kingdom Publishers

Kingdom Publishers
London, UK.

You can purchase copies of this book from any leading bookstore or email **contact@kingdompublishers.co.uk**

To my dear sister Leila

Dr. S. K. Haddad was born in Palestine to Lebanese parents. His family moved to Lebanon in 1948. He studied Medicine and Surgery at the Universities of Cambridge and London, and specialized in Neurosurgery. He is now retired and lives in Wales.

This book of poetry is of Christian poems, but there are some of nature and other aspects of life that are important to the Christian. Many of the poems have been previously published in other books together with topics of life and death, nature, conflict, and love. There is a good number of new poems in this book that have not been published before.

TABLE OF CONTENTS

Creation	13
The Universe	17
The River	19
The Moon	21
The Volcano	23
The Seasons	24
Winter	24
Snow showers	26
The Robin	27
Spring	29
The Blackbird	31
The Fledgling	33
Summer	35
Sunset	37
First Light	39
Sunrise	40
Autumn	42
The Galilean Storm	44
The Widow of Nain	45
The Woman with an Issue of Blood	47
Hagar	49
While on the Cross	51
Lazarus	52
The Crucifixion of Christ	54

Praise	56
Thee Holy Spirit	57
Christian Martyrdom	58
Redemption	59
Satan Defeated	60
Unbelief	61
Persecution	62
The Healing of a Woman	64
The Virgin Mother	66
Rizpah	68
Spiritual Blindness	69
Peniel	70
Joseph	72
Deathbed	74
Rahab	75
The Unbeliever	77
On the Sea Shore	79
The Fall	81
A Fallen World	82
The Hurricane	88
The Rape of Kuwait - August 1990	90
Mankind	92
The Invasion of Kuwait	96
Africa	99
Man's Will	100
There is None Righteous	102
Providence	103
Bondage	104
Advent	105
Bethlehem	106

Repentance	107
Like Seagulls	108
The Atheist's Faith	109
No Beauty Oil	112
Folly	113
Pride	115
At Twilight	117
The Oppressed	119
Freedom	120
The Village Church	122
Death of a Christian Lady	125
Death is Swallowed up in Victory	127
The Tree	130
When Jesus Died	132
Loneliness	134
Condescension	136
Dishonoured	138
The Crucified	139
Salvation	142
Sacrifice	144
Christ Conquered	145
Bearer of my Sin	146
Foe Me	147
O Sword of God	149
Consecration	150
A Plea	151
The Red Card	153
Blind Bartimeus	154
The Blind Child	156
Alfred	158

When Time Trampled on her Head	160
Life	162
The Reaper	164
Not Tonight	165
The Fall of Babylon - 536 B.C.	166
Judgment	167
Hell	169
Injustice	170
Christ Will Remember	173
The Last Day	176
Morning Prayer	179
Evening Prayer	181

CREATION

"In the beginning God created the heaven and the earth"
(Genesis 1:1).

Hosts of Heaven, observe and see
How time and space will come to be,
Will run their course by God's decree.

God Almighty will surely act
To form a world, perfect, intact,
With dimensions of south and north:
Out of nothing it will spring forth;
New worlds will spin before your eyes
When Earth is born with shining skies.

Blinding light emanates with might,
Shatters the darkness of the night:
It rises from its nascent sleep
To flood the darkness of the deep
And usher in the first day morn,
Particles of matter are born
Packed with energy bearing fire,
Held in a primeval sapphire
From which the seas and stars will form,
Bright green fields and magnetic storm.
Thus it was in creation's sway:
When light burst forth on the first day.

Winds and waves churned in the abyss
Waited to receive Heaven's kiss
And properly divided in twain
With heaven's water to remain
Until such time as God sends down
The Flood to cause the Earth to drown.
Thus it was in creations sway:
Firmaments rose the second day.

Gather great waters, form the seas,
Island project, let the tall trees
Upon your multicoloured land,
Upon your naked breast to stand.
Thus it was upon the third day
That mountains, great in every way,
Towered toward the cloudless sky,
Hugged by the cold wind passing by;
Trees, laden with succulent fruits,
Were held by earth-bound branching roots;
Flowers of Paradise, most fair,
Distilled their fragrance through the air;
Seed-bearing plants, all dressed with green,
Sprang up to compliment the scene.
While rivers coursing through the land
Caressed the rocks, the clay, the sand.
Thus it was in creation's sway:
Green Earth appeared on the third day.

Securely held by God's right hand
Energy fulfilled His demand,
Budding forth to firmly uphold
The galaxies which did unfold.
It was when God opened His fist
That stars floated in the deep mist,
Countless as all the sea shore's sand:
Awesome power does God command!

In heaven's vault, to shine from high,
The sun and moon and stars did fly;
Silently watched the world below,
Gave it their light and warming glow.
Thus it was in creation's sway:
Heaven was lit on the fourth day.

And then life in the oceans teemed:
Shark and dolphin in friendship teamed;
Whitebait, salmon and mighty whale
Swam through the weeds, dark green and pale.
And in the sea the fishes breathed
While waters rushed and burst and seethed.
Then in the air birds took to wing;
They were endowed with skill to sing
And in the shades of sunlit hue
They drank of the fifth morning dew;
Their throats sounded the tunes of praise,
Their feathers gleamed in splendid ways.
Thus it was in creation's sway:
Sea and air lived on the fifth day.

The sixth day saw animals appear:
The lion, tiger, bear, and deer,
Leaping, walking with varied stance
Joined calf and lamb and wolf in dance;
Upon this novel earthly scene,
Horses trotted, cattle were seen.
It was upon the last sixth day
That of primeval muddy clay,
God's ultimate action was wrought
When He shaped man with careful thought
Of clay, and His own breath, by hand,
Upright in bearing, free to stand
And from the first day of his birth
Was made possessor of the Earth,

To be to God a faithful friend,
Power, wisdom, reason to blend.
Thus it was in creation's sway:
Creation's end was the sixth day.

In this newly created world,
Wondrous beauty, budded, unfurled;
Peace and harmony reigned supreme:
There was no death in land or stream;
Big fish did not consume the small;
The weeds and herbs were food for all;
Man and beasts and birds of feather
Preyed not the one on the other.

Rejoice angels, God's mighty works
Made creatures where His splendour lurks.
Who beside Him can combine
Fission, fusion to intertwine?
Or let energy be confined
In star, insect, and human mind?
No man can ever search to know
The intricate world here below
Or heavens with their store of fire:
Who can to the great One aspire?
Thus it was in creation's sway:
God rested on the seventh day.

THE UNIVERSE

The stars float in the silence
Of the farthest wide expanse;
The wheels of eternity
Dance a noiseless, skilful dance.
Keep the balance of nature
In a perfect, flawless stance.

Observe the scattered clusters
Unfathomed in their high place,
Who can fathom what distance
Separates each splendent face
In the eternal embrace
Of the spacious globe of space.

They run their course faithfully
With a quartz-like precision,
Steadfast in constant motion,
Free of wayward division;
Planets encircle their masses
With no chance of collision.

The fire of stunning fusions
Illuminates the vast deep:
Giant flaming tongues arise
With a bold and mighty sweep
Lick the outer edge of space
Then fall to their source and creep.

Oceans of light are seething
With a fantastic splendour;
Can language ever describe
The incandescent wonder?
Yet the timeless stars received
The force which they engender.

Masses which burst with fury
Became deserts where they lie,
Of gases shown by starlight
From furnaces far and nigh,
Like the Crab, not fully formed
Which cannot mangle the sky.

Dispersed in emptiness,
Covered in a shroud of black,
Float the gaseous nebulae
With many a hidden track,
Riding in the endless deep
Like the Horse without a back.

The universe is finite,
Its borders are well hidden;
A shining mulberry tree
With burning fruit, forbidden;
A branch is seen in our sky:
A Milk trail yet untrodden.

It spins in part and in whole
By the wheels of eternity driven;
Spiral galaxies, starfish
Rotate in distant heaven;
The great energy of space
Was by our great God given.

THE RIVER

Flow, river, gently flow
To the waiting lands below,
Through thirsty fields and meadows
Meander as maid and beau;
Be friend to trees and shadows
Scatter coolness as you flow:
Leave noisy busy cities,
Follow seagulls where they go.

Restore the heat-parched furrows
With moisture you bestow;
Greet the newborn grazing lambs
And whisper to them, hello!
Fill the deep vales and gorges,
Let your splendid beauty show,
Let the young trout and salmon
Increase in number and grow.

At the dawn of creation,
Before man first used the hoe,
You nourished the trees of Eden
Then standing firm row in row
And you peacefully glittered
In the setting sun aglow,
While the crystal waterfalls
Leapt with the charm of a doe.

Son of the springs in the mountain,
Of the highest peaks of snow,
Of lakes, marshes the fountain

Where lovers learn love to know,
Born in honour, yet humbly
Working the earth lying low
Where the swan rides on your back
And where the salt air breezes blow.

Undulating the mainstream
A serpent, here fast, there slow;
Waters run into your heart
To sustain the goose, the crow;
Branches spread out in the land
To bid the farmers to sow:
To trust that life will return
 As in the wet sky, the bow.

Roll, mighty ageless river,
Born many years ago;
Let not the grassland quiver,
Rise not to become its foe;
Bring, not demise, destruction,
Bring rich blessings, not the woe;
Embrace the waiting ocean,
Losing yourself as you flow.

THE MOON

Arise to announce a month returned,
Circle the Earth while kingdoms are burned:
From yonder height you observed all,
The rise of empires and their downfall.

Command the fine movement of the sea,
Of the mighty waves, seemingly free,
Cause the ebbing, flowing of the tide
In early morn and at eventide.

Then show men your young and crescent face
As in the heavens you run your race
With Venus happily at your side,
Proud to look on, unwilling to hide.

Silently rising, in silence set,
Wooing the soul to weep and forget,
Symbol of nations in the vast East,
Signal to start the fast and the feast.

Slowly grow into a shining sphere,
Engender beauty, dispel the fear,
Guardian of lovers, guardian of love,
Light to the wayfarer from above.

Banish the starlight from the sky,
Climb up the mountain, ascend on high,
Preserve a corner as black as tar
Where men can espy a distant star.

Slowly diminish, then rest in sleep,
Let darkness overwhelm the deep,
Return anew to let mortal man
Number the short days of his life span.

Worshipped by many in days of yore,
A symbol of fear and of folklore,
Yet God's laws engulf you and surround
Your waxing, waning and awesome ground.

Your pock-scarred face awaited to greet
Man who trampled your head with his feet,
Peering into your craters he raised
A cry from a soul truly amazed.

In lonely silence, aloof, remote,
Sail on in heaven's ocean, a boat,
Far from the noises of mother Earth,
From the cry of men at death and birth.

THE VOLCANO

The mountain stands in glory, resplendent and high
Nudging the vault of heaven through the clouds and sky,
Hiding its dreadful fury, watching man and beast,
Churning its bubbling bowels like the hops with yeast
Waiting in heated ferment for its sound to rise
Much like the roar of battle through the watching skies.

Waiting with bated patience, boiling like the broth,
It will exile the silence in its fearful wrath,
Homes with kitchen lights burning live the weary day,
Men from their toil returning hurry on their way,
Their wives and children yearning to welcome their eyes
As the great darkness thickens in the anxious skies.

The dormant sun is rising in the darkest hours
While thunderclaps are bursting with blazing showers,
The sleeping giant waking from slumber, too deep,
Belches out hot fury on the mountain steep,
Arise, O weary bodies from your well-earned sleep,
Desert your homes and treasures before the fires creep.

Hurry up, my sister, leave your dolls and run,
Scatter away, my children, from the burning sun,
The mountain top is melting with fountains aflame,
Lord, in Your care abiding, do not blot out our name.
Great is the force of nature, who is strong to stand?
The molten stream gently flows to cover the land.

THE SEASONS

"While the earth remaineth: seedtime and harvest, and cold and heat, and summer and winter, and day and night shall not cease" (Genesis 8:22).

WINTER

As if the night has come to stay,
Tall is the darkness, short the day,
The biting wind does howl and bray.

The earth does wear a dress of white,
But when the sun sheds forth its light,
Man forgets the nearness of night.

The cattle feed on bales of hay,
The grass is covered in the brae,
Horses within the stables neigh.

As if the clouds, from distant height
Fell down upon the earth outright
To cloth the fields and trees in sight.

Some sit beside teapot and tray
Watching the fire burn away
Until the world warms one Spring day.

Man does not cease to work and fight
Against the storms and floods that blight
His dwellings with ferocious might.

He will rise up one day and pray
And plead with his Maker to stay
His hand lest death reveals the way.

Feeble his strength and great his plight,
He does not know his left from right
When nature's forces strike and bite.

He longs to see the month of May
When newborn chicks hatch out to play,
When sunshine might adorn his way.

With thoughts that give his heart delight
And dreams which feed his appetite,
He whiles away the Winter's night.

SNOW SHOWERS

The sun smiles at the crispy air,
Snow flakes, like my grandfather's hair
Fall on the lady in the street
Walking slowly with frozen feet,
Wrapped up in tweed coat, scarf and hat
To buy food for herself and cat.

Today's showers are full of snow,
Woollen tufts float to earth below,
Driven, like locusts, they come down
Upon foreheads which hide and frown,
Which show annoyance when they feel
Kisses from lips of icy steel.

The down scatters from the white dove,
Fingers are numb inside the glove,
The red nose hangs a drop of dew,
The mouth puffs steam from heated stew,
The young, though covered, feel the cold,
What of the infirm and the old?

THE ROBIN

It never sang in a choir
Although properly dressed
Wearing the red shield of fire
Upon its little breast.

Its twig-like limbs are nimble,
Its hopping, firm in style,
The measure of a thimble
Sustains it for a while.

Its posture, straight, an arrow,
A rocket of the skies,
And tiny bones and marrow
Add grandeur when it flies.

When men dig up their gardens
It comes with a soft chirm
Before the turned soil hardens
To snatch a wriggling worm.

When standing by a flower
It steals the splendid scene,
While in the shady bower
Excels the shades of green.

Not bound by man's religion
Yet lives by nature's creed
A friend to the wild pigeon,
But lacks its fervent greed.

In snows of hardest winter
Picks at a lonely bough,
Its weight as on a splinter
Makes it to gently bow.

Its life is short and fleeting,
But never fails to please,
Many a Christmas greeting
Shows it midst snows and trees.

SPRING

The raging storms and tempests, their fury at last abated,
The earth by tears of heaven was nourished and satiated,
The roaring drums of thunder are worn out and deflated.

The bustling wind retreated before the face of the breeze,
It is time for tenderness to caress the gentle trees,
Let them sway with majesty, with splendid skill and ease.

The sleeping bud was wakened by a singing bird,
It looked into the thicket from where the squeaking was heard
To find that a new hatched life and a newborn song were shared.

The rose washed its face with dew then slowly opened its eyes,
Saw the sphere of shining light in blue and glistening skies,
Caused its enchanting fragrance above the green hills to rise.

Bees, not knowing any shame, lustily kiss the flowers,
Trade fertile seed for nectar amidst the scattered showers,
Not hustled by sun or rain from dawn till evening hours.

Spring has returned, the beloved, by all nature awaited,
The day of rebirth has come, not one day belated,
Flowers greet in the soil, in back yard walls, not slated.

Renewed nature is giving in friendship its vibrant hand,
Calling the fields and meadows, the happy and budding land,
Asking men to ponder, behold its beauty, now grand.

The days of cold and darkness, of hardship, severe and deep
Retreat to allow men's dreams and fresh hopes to gently creep
Now that life has awakened from disturbed and restless sleep.

THE BLACKBIRD

Blackbird in my small garden,
Who fashioned you charcoal black?
Who made your feathers glisten
That water runs off your back?
Who made your fine beak golden
To carry and pick and crack?
Your beauty ever charms me,
Far greater than a greyback.

You stand in graceful manner
Looking for a hidden snare,
Much like a waving banner,
But listening to the air;
I see you timid, cautious,
Fearful to approach, to dare;
Come down, partake of plenty
While in the Almighty's care.

How deep is your chirping sound,
Almost pretending to speak!
You come for a nibbling bite
Then hurry to fill your beak
To feed your few hidden ones
Whose bodies are small and sleek,
Unable to search for food
While growing stronger each week.

Who taught art for building?
A safe nest of twigs and straw?

To keep your little fledglings
From predator and foe?
When you see harm approaching,
You most assuredly know;
Your instinct flares and rises
Like an arrow from the bow.

You bring your young ones to visit
My small garden in the spring;
Their little feathers flutter
Excited by food you bring.
I see them grow in fatness
Till bravely they take to wing;
I hear their high pitched squeaking:
They do their utmost to sing.

Blackbird, you go, I miss you,
Your offspring the take your place.
Where do you hide when lonely,
When death submerges your face?
I fail to find your body
Amidst the branches I trace;
My God, who made and taught you,
Will keep you in his embrace.

THE FLEDGLING

It was crouching against the garden wall
As from its safe nest it suffered a fall,
The blackbird fledgling seemed ready to die,
Unable to cry, unable to call.

Within five minutes it lay on the ground
With heaving breast, yet not making a sound,
It seemed that quite soon it will breathe its last,
Its short life waning, while its heart drums pound.

 A moving hand approached to hold its frame
And save it from becoming a live game
To prowling cats that bite and toss and kill
A helpless creature, both wounded and lame.

It suddenly moved and took to the street,
Beating its frail wings, running on its feet,
The hand chased it with skill lest it becomes
A crushed smudge of feathers and pale raw meat.

When it was captured it tried hard to bite
The hand that held it with kindness, not spite,
Which in the shade of the garden shrubs it placed
The little fledgling, overcome with fright.

And suddenly, out of nowhere, there came
A mother blackbird, like a jealous dame
That stood and stared to see whether he was
A pitying friend or a man of shame.

Nature will take its course, it is best
That one can do and leave the mind to rest,
The mother will care for its offspring's good
And God is praised and magnified and blest.

SUMMER

The shortest day is lost in night,
The longest day comes into sight,
The sun sleeps in a bed of light.

The stars peeped early in the sky,
Now are reluctant, bashful, shy,
The full moon smiles at the firefly.

Reaching its full maturity,
Pregnant Nature, with dignity,
Begets her child, Fertility.

Golden chandeliers, green and red
Hang in vineyard and proud homestead
While wheat is ripe for making bread.

The heavy fruit weighs down the boughs,
Pastures abound with sheep and cows,
A true man thanks his God and bows.

Strolling blissfully, hand in hand
Facing the unknown, bleak or grand,
Young lovers walk in their dreamland.

As if the whole of life is theirs,
Where are troubles, annoying cares
When the warm sun looks down and stares?

All people bless the Summer's day,
The time of mirth and holiday
And wish that it will always stay.

But when the leaves shed their brown leaves,
Summer feels cold without its sleeves:
It quickly packs its bag and leaves.

SUNSET

Billions, billions tiny atoms
Join together and explode
To scatter to man a blessing
Wherever his abode;
Though awesome in widest fury
Man's heart does not forebode:
The hydrogen atoms fusing
Upon high heaven's road
Are subject to the Almighty
Whose hands bind and encode
The great atom's finite power,
Its energy and mode.

The star, one of a myriad stars
Runs swiftly to the west,
Leaving the lazy eastern shore,
Calling for men to rest,
Exposing its fiery body
With naked, shining breast
To plunge into the water's depth
With urgent speed and zest;
Birds vainly follow where it sleeps
To build themselves a nest.

As if the seaman's hand can reach
To touch the ball of fire
Falling into the ocean's mouth
Out of the deep sapphire;

No sizzling is heard, no steam seen,
No waves rising higher;
The sea grows cold,
Should it not boil
To bring forth blood and mire
When the horizon is crimson
Like a flaming brier?

The creatures of the night awake,
To them the day is born.
In many souls a fire is lit
With memories reborn,
While others in darkness cower,
In loneliness to mourn,
Awaiting anxiously the light
To usher in the morn
That hope may join with tenderness
Their hearts, broken and torn.

Life is governed by its sure course,
Mother of radiant rays;
Man counts its journey in the sky
To number all his days.

FIRST LIGHT

While darkness covers dark and green
And night creatures frolic unseen;
When sleeping men begin to toss
And frogs jump high amidst the moss,
The night prepares to flee from sight
Like clouds that vanish in the night,
Like a whiff of smoke, blown away
To make room for another day.

Creeping on tiptoes in the dark,
Calling sparrow, robin, and lark,
The night stretches its neck headlong
To be greeted by chirping song;
It enters slowly from beyond
Uncovers mountain, plain, and pond;
The darkness runs, it leaves no mark
While waking dogs begin to bark.

SUNRISE

The sun's herald will soon awake
To announce the new daybreak
But the heralds of the morning
Warble while the day is yawning.

The dark carries the marks of night
Its darkened face unwashed by light
Until the dawn drinks of the dew,
Paves the day for the sun anew.

But when the light shines on its face
It marches with a gentle pace
To make way for the early morn:
Travail ended, the day is born.

The mighty star will then appear
To shine forth if the sky is clear,
To turn the sky to gold and red
When stepping from its glowing bed.

When it shines above still waters
A mirror blinks in all quarters
While in the desert's pure sapphire
Its flame ignites the furnace fire.

It moves with majesty, a king
To shelter earth under its wing
With precious gifts of light and heat
That men and beasts may live and eat.

It is God's messenger of peace
That life may flourish and increase
But man has forgotten God's ways
And hardly thanks Him for its rays.

AUTUMN

It has returned to boldly say,
Farewell to warmth, to Summer's day,
To herald the night on its way.

They fall, meander through the air,
They lost their grip and lost their glare,
The leaves have left the tall trees bare.

Time came to wound them and to tear,
It held them, held me in its snare
And turned to grey my ageing hair.

The sun has travelled far away,
The cold and darkness hold their sway
On man and beast and freezing clay.

Migrating birds now fill the sky,
Warbling their sombre tune on high,
Yearning for warm lands as they fly.

Come, creatures, make your bed to sleep
Before the winds blow hard and sweep;
Earthworms, in dungeons hide and creep.

Many observe that life is lent,
Their numbered days are almost spent,
Foreboding strikes a spirit bent.

Sadness rises, despair is nigh,
The soul trembles as time runs by
That with all nature it will die.

Corruption marches with its woe,
Death comes to reap and plough and sow,
Even the brave will cry out, No!

Man fears dissolution, and squirms,
He will accept all offered terms,
Is the last triumph for the worms?

He clings to life with braided string,
Wonders what each new day will bring
While yearning for the scent of Spring.

Though branches break and twigs will fall,
Though Death comes wearing its black shawl,
Eternity is man's last call.

THE GALILEAN STORM

"Peace, be still" (Mark 4:39)

The wind was raging, the men were fretful
And Jesus was asleep;
The boat was filling, the men were fearful
Of sinking in the deep.

They rushed to wake Him and then accused Him
O showing no care;
How can you thus sleep, we are near the brim
Of a watery snare.

The Lord promptly rose, commanded the sea
And said, "Peace be still";
The wind subsided and then Galilee
Was calm and very still.

The disciples said, what kind of a man
Whose word the winds obey?
No one is able and nobody can
Command the sea any day.

Little did they know, that with them asleep
Was God whose strong arm
Created all things, and will surely keep
His own from all harm.

THE WIDOW Of NAIN

"Weep not" (Luke 7:13)

She wept and wailed and deeply cried
Because her only son had died;
Poor widow of the town of Nain,
Her boy will not come home again.

They carried him toward the tomb,
The one she nourished in her womb;
Distraught, helpless and full of pain,
Poor widow of the town of Nain.

But the Lord Jesus passed that way
And he had pity straight away;
Approached and said, "weep not", to her:
A thing that seemed to mock her care.

Then Jesus touched the bier of wood;
The procession stopped where it stood,
And with majesty and might,
He spoke to the dead man outright.

"Young man, I say to you, arise",
He sat and spoke, to their surprise.
The compassion the Lord had shown
Would even melt a heart of stone.

The Lord of life, the gentle dove,
The Lord of pity, grace and love,
Our Saviour, Jesus Christ the Lord,
Even the dead obey His word.

THE WOMAN WITH AN ISSUE OF BLOOD

"Daughter, thy faith hath made thee whole" (Mark 5:34).

She touched the hem of His raiment
 Believing that at that moment
Her issue of bad blood would cease
While she remained concealed, at ease.

For twelve years she suffered bleeding
And this was her life impeding
As she was regarded unclean:
A social outcast she had been.

But she heard of Jesus passing
And her courage was amassing
To get what doctors could not give
To make her clean and really live.

Jesus felt some virtue leave Him,
Turned and asked the men around Him:
Who has touched my raiment? He said,
And the woman was full of dread.

His disciples saw that the crowd
Was around Him, noisy and loud,
Some pushing others to be near,
Some unbelieving, some sincere.

'How can You say, who has touched Me
When the masses, countless and free
Are thronging you, themselves asserting?'
Thus were His disciples blurting.

The woman came trembling and afraid,
Confessing that it was she who laid
Her hand on the hem of his gown
And having said that, she looked down.

The Lord was gracious to assure
The maid whose trust in Him was sure
"Daughter, your faith has made you whole,
Go in peace", be healed in your soul.

The Lord's compassion is so great,
His mercy too vast to abate
There is none like Him midst humankind,
Tender, loving and very kind.

HAGAR

"What aileth thee, Hagar" (Genesis 21:17)

She was removed from her master's homestead,
Given for the journey water and bread,
Hagar in the wilderness with her son
Roamed weary and sad with no hope, not one.

The eastern sun was harsh upon the land,
Neither she nor Ishmael could withstand
The dreadful heat in the empty terrain
With none to help them and none to sustain.

Hagar, Abraham's maid and concubine,
A bondslave whose son did undermine
Sarah's child, Isaac, as he chose to sneer
At his younger brother of fewer years,

They wandered in the wilderness, half dead,
Weary and not knowing where the road led,
The water was spent and there was no shade,
Her son weakened, was under a bush laid.

Distraught, she said, I cannot see him die
And she stood away and began to cry,
But God from His heaven heard the lad groan
For to Him all things that happen are known.

"What ails you, Hagar, fear not" said the Lord -
The merciful One is of faithful word -
Lift up the boy and hold him with your hand,
I shall make him a nation, a great band.

She opened her eyes and saw a water well,
Filled up the bottle and his thirst did quell
And God was with them and the lad did grow
To be an archer with a mighty bow.

WHILE ON THE CROSS

"Behold thy son!" (John 19:26).

His mother stood at the foot of the cross
And John, the disciple too;
She wept as she viewed her tremendous loss:
There was nothing they could do.

Despite the pain of His body and soul
Jesus saw His mother there;
Amidst the torment of the blood and gall
He had a kind word for her.

He looked at her and said, "Behold your son"
The one who was dear to Me;
To John He said, "See your mother", the one
That highly cherished should be.

Who can imagine that any would do
What the dying Lord had done:
He safeguarded His mother, her life too
Before His own life was gone.

LAZARUS

"Lazarus, come forth" (John 11:43)

They sent to Jesus, pleading, and said,
The one you love is sick in bed,
His life hangs on a tiny thread.

Jesus tarried and did not go
To ease their misery and woe,
For He knew what they could not know.

They wept for their brother who died
And in their sadness, wailed and cried
And the hot tears could not be dried.

They washed the body of the dead;
Wrapped in linen from foot to head,
It was placed in the grave of dread.

When Jesus showed they put the blame
On him, for if He quickly came,
The outcome would not be the same.

"I am the resurrection and life",
Said Jesus, whose power was rife
To deal with awesome death and life.

He saw Martha and Mary weep,
His compassion, was strong and deep,
That Jesus then began to weep.

He said to them, "remove the stone",
But four days dead, his stink alone
Would stifle any to the bone.

And, with authority, the Word
Cried to the dead, and the crowd heard,
"Lazarus, come forth", was His word.

And the dead walked out, enshrouded
To the sunlight that was crowded
And to life again unbounded.

The Lord has majesty and might,
Conqueror of death and of night,
And is the everlasting light.

THE CRUCIFIXION OF CHRIST

*"And when they were come to the place, which is called Calvary,
there they crucified him"* (Luke 23:33).

Pilate pronounced Him innocent
Yet gave Him up to die,
And, in truth, was God's instrument
For he could crucify.

The daughters of Jerusalem
Offered Him myrrh and wine
And in the turbulent mayhem
Our Saviour did decline.

Would not be drugged to ease the pain
Of gross and cruel death
Upon the cross that was the bane
Of yielding up His breath.

And the whole people mocked and jeered
At Him, a dying man;
They praised one another and cheered
That they fulfilled their plan.

There was no one who showed pity:
They railed at Him, on the cross,
Wagging their heads, grudging, gritty:
To them He was no loss.

He feared not pain or suffering
Nor that they scathed His name,
But that He was an offering
For all our sin and shame.

The Father's wrath was directed
On Him till He was claimed
By death, when scorned and rejected
And hurt, punished and maimed.

Lord Jesus, You alone carried
Our burden and our guilt
And were crucified and harried
Until Your blood was spilt.

For the joy that was before You:
The people You Redeemed,
You rose and gave them life anew
And is by them esteemed.

Out of the travail of Your soul
You set Your people free,
 Your tender love has made them whole:
Satisfied You shall be.

PRAISE

"There is joy in the presence of the angels of God over one sinner that repenteth" (Luke 15:10).

We praise God, the eternal One
With loud and cheering voice
For His great salvation was done
And in Him we rejoice.

He left us not to die in sin,
But saved us by His grace
And has renewed us from within
To run a holy race.

The angels sang, shouted with joy
When time and space were born;
Much more their voices will employ
When man to God is drawn.

What love, what mercy He has shown
To bruise the Christ, that we,
Restored and saved should be His own
For God, the One in Three.

THE HOLY SPIRIT

Great Spirit of the living God,
Forever worshipped and adored,
Eternal life, of life the Lord,
Under Your care we thrive and live.

Giver of inner life and peace,
Our wills, to holiness, increase,
Our sins subdue, our ills decrease
With help that only You can give.

May we not grieve You nor betray
Your gentle love and holy way,
Abide with us, let us not stray,
Be by our side, our sins forgive.

God of all truth and holiness,
Guide of our lives in weariness,
Open Your word, with joyfulness
And righteousness our souls shall live.

CHRISTIAN MARTYRDOM

"And fear not them which kill the body, but are not able to kill the soul, but rather fear him which is able to destroy both soul and body in hell" (Matthew 10:28).

How dreadful is the wrath of man:
He slaughters whenever he can
The innocents, and their blood ran
Upon the grass, and desert sand.

It is most natural to fear
The killing that ignores the tear,
The hacking with machete and spear
As Christians are slain where they stand.

I think that in that final hour,
The Holy Spirit, of great power
Gives them courage not to cower
And, in faithfulness, to withstand.

The slayer cannot kill the soul,
Only the body, not the whole;
God will destroy him and enthral
In hell, with no relief at hand.

REDEMPTION

"In whom we have redemption through his blood"
(Ephesians 1:7).

Lord Jesus, You purchased my soul;
I was drowning in sin's dark hole
And Your own blood was shed for me.
I can't but love you and adore
For You have loved me first, much more
And died for me upon the tree.

You redeemed me, You redeemed me,
From eternal death redeemed me
And now I am guiltless, free.
My sin was on You when You died,
When, with a mighty voice, You cried,
It is done, to God the payee.

The Spirit raised You from the dead
And You became the Church's head,
Her Prophet, Priest and King always.
Our debt to You is vast to trace,
And one day we shall see Your face
And then, forever, sing Your praise.

SATAN DEFEATED

"The Son of God was manifested, that he might destroy the works of the devil" (1John 3:8).

When we in Adam went astray,
Did not listen, did not obey,
Satan was pleased he won the day.

He thought he spoiled God's world for aye,
Treated mankind with lie on lie,
Worked to kill Christ and see Him die.

He was ignorant of God's plan,
That by Christ's death, God would save man
And thus he lost the fight and ran.

By His death and resurrection,
Christ has saved us to perfection,
Condemned Satan to destruction.

UNBELIEF

"But though he had done so many miracles before them, yet they believed not on him" (John 12:37).

Unbelief is beyond belief
However sincere it may be;
There is no cure and no relief
But grace and mercy, deep and free.

They saw Christ heal the sick and lame
And raise the dead, the Pharisees,
They should, with joy, have blessed His name
And worshipped Him, bowing the knee.

They said He was devil possessed,
A madman, unworthy to live;
They mocked Him and were not impressed
By love and peace that He could give.

Unbelief is foolish, unwise,
Cannot behold what could be seen;
 God only can open blind eyes
To see the wonder of the scene.

PERSECUTION

"But he that denieth me before men shall be denied before the angels of God" (Luke 12:9).

O Lord of majesty and might
Whose holiness excels the light
To whom the angels sing their praise;
We glory in Your perfect work
From which our Saviour did not shirk
To die for us, our sins erase.

"In the beginning was the Word"
Whose Spirit in God is the third
Where truth and majesty combine;
Giver of life, as God sees fit,
Honouring Christ in every whit,
Eternal God, holy, divine.

Descend on us, Spirit, descend,
Let us with helping hand attend
To men and women, poor, oppressed;
To bring the gospel and to aid
Their plight where sinful men invade
Their freedom and leave them distressed.

We think of those who went before,
True heroes of the faith and more
Whose eyes were gouged, and their skin flayed
While others, boiled in oil or burned
Or beheaded yet had not turned
From their just Redeemer, but prayed.

O give us courage so that we
True and loyal will ever be
To suffer hardship and to die
Like Your own people in the world,
Persecuted and truly scared
Of death, though You are ever nigh.

Jesus Himself suffered and died
For our sins that shouted and cried
Against us to a holy God;
His agony was great and keen,
Nothing like it had ever been,
He bravely endured Heaven's rod.

May we not deny Him ever;
And be unfaithful and sever
Our closest fellowship with Him;
Let us bear the cross and be led
To what it means: place of the dead,
Weeping and yet singing a hymn.

THE HEALING OF A WOMAN

"Woman, thou art loosed from thine infirmity" (Luke 13:12).

Poor woman, was bent for eighteen years,
Unable to look up to the sky,
Only the ground was within her sphere,
Could not see a person, eye to eye.

Lord Jesus was teaching in her church:
A synagogue where they learnt the law;
He saw her coming, His eyes did search
Her inward self, her sorrow and woe.

He called her to Him and promptly said:
You are now loosed from that which binds you,
Then He touched her and she raised her head,
Praised God and gave Him the glory due.

The Lord healed her on the Sabbath day
Which angered the ruler of that place,
A coward, who then began to say,
Come and be healed on six other days.

The Lord did not stay silent and said,
Your ox is loosed on the Sabbath day,
Hypocrite, and to water is led,
And this poor woman is loosed today.

The man was shamed with the like-minded,
The people rejoiced at the event;
Perhaps the synagogue was crowded
And the crowd's gladness none could prevent.

What sadness that compassion has died
In men's heart who interpret the law
As they please caring not if one cried
In bondage to ill, cruel and raw.

THE VIRGIN MOTHER

The power of the Highest shall overshadow thee" (Luke 1:35).

Most favoured woman on the earth,
A humble Galilean maid,
Chosen to give the Saviour birth
When, in her womb, He would be laid.

The angel Gabriel was sent
To give her news of her first child;
She listened to him, her ear lent
For she was lowly, meek and mild.

"How can I ever have a son
When I have never known a man?"
'God's own Spirit, the Holy One
Shall descend on you in God's plan'.

Gladly engaged to a just man,
She would be with child out of time;
How could he, or anyone can
Not abandon her for her crime?

Mary, most blessed of womankind
Did not fear of being disgraced,
Surrendered to the One most kind
Who was near, whatever she faced.

And she meekly took on the role
Of being mother to the Christ
And submitted to God her all,
A great action of faith, unpriced.

"Behold the handmaid of the Lord"
Was her sure and trusting reply
To the great angel and his word,
For upon God she did rely.

How little she did foreknow then
That wicked men will crucify
Her son, who for women and men
Will shed his sacred blood and die.

RIZPAH

"Suffered neither the birds of the air to rest on them by day, nor the beasts of the field by night" (2Samuel 21:10).

Her sons were slain, then on a gibbet hung;
On her house, the arrows of death were flung;
She was bereaved and did nothing but mourn
While tears of blood from her heart were wrung.

She guarded their corpses all night and day,
Kept them from wild birds that she pushed away
And in the night, the wild beasts came to feed,
But she kept her sons from falling a prey.

Tender mother, noble woman and rare
Who placed herself at risk, but did not care;
The stench and ugly sight did not disturb
This, most gracious woman, nor did they scare.

King David heard of Rizpah and her deed,
Leapt to alleviate her sorrow and need;
He buried her sons with their father's bones
In grandfather's grave: a mercy indeed.

Rizpah's name, little known, but will remain
A sign of tender love, and that is plain;
She was Saul's concubine and she was named
In the Scriptures in Saul's and David's reign.

SPIRITUAL BLINDNESS

"They have a zeal of God, but not according to knowledge"
(Romans 10:2).

They sent Him to die by crucifixion,
The Christ who came to bless them and to save
And to remove from them all affliction,
But they had Him allotted to the grave.

The Christ for whom they had waited for years,
Whom they failed to recognize when He came,
Came to redeem them with His blood and tears,
But they rejected Him and cursed His name.

He healed their sick, drove out devils and more,
Raised the dead whom they saw with their blind eyes,
Comforted the weary, their troubles bore,
Yet they despised Him with deceit and lies.

O Israel, you killed your Messiah,
You derided and had Him crucified,
But He fulfilled the words of Isaiah
And as a sin offering He suffered and died.

Trust the Redeemer, repent and believe
Him whom the grave was not able to hold;
Eternal life, the gift you will receive
Will be yours with many blessings untold.

PENIEL

"Thy name shall be called no more Jacob, but Israel: for as a prince hast thou power with God and with men, and hast prevailed" (Genesis 32:28). "He wept, and made supplication unto him" (Hosea 12:4).

Dreading the day and full of fear,
Jacob spent the whole night alone
With foreboding as he was near
One he held by the anklebone.

For Esau marched with fighting men
To the brother who cheated him,
Stole the blessing and straightway then
Escaped lest his fate be grim.

But God would not leave him alone:
A man wrestled him all the night
Until the breaking of the dawn
And the appearing of the light.

The man touched Jacob on his thigh
And Jacob limped, but would not yield;
He wrestled on, though he did cry,
But was his equal in the field.

He said to Jacob, let me go
For the new day is breaking now,
Not till you bless me for I know
That your blessing you must endow.

He answered then, what is your name?
It is Jacob, he promptly said;
You fought with God and overcame:
Israel is your name instead.

He blessed him at the break of day,
Jacob said, I have seen God's face;
Leaned on his staff and went away,
At peace, ready for Esau's face.

When Esau saw him he did run
And hugged and kissed the long-gone twin:
Hatred and vengeance have now gone,
He invited to Seir his kin.

JOSEPH

"I have dreamed a dream and there is none that can interpret it" (Genesis 41:15).

He lingered in prison through no fault of his own,
But through a woman whose web of lies she had sewn:
Married to his master, but still desired a slave
To know her in a way his own master had known.

Pharaoh's butler and baker were imprisoned then;
One night, each dreamed a dream that was beyond his ken,
The next morning saw them depressed and very sad
With misery showing on these two blighted men.

Joseph enquired of them and they both then said:
We had a troublesome dream, perhaps of the dead,
We know not what they mean, but they have made their mark
And have brought to our hearts a most foreboding dread.

Tell me what you saw, he said, and I will explain,
For man cannot interpret, but God makes it plain.
The butler said, a three branched vine blossomed and grew,
I pressed the grapes and gave Pharaoh his cup again.

Then Joseph said, in three days you will be restored
To give Pharaoh the cup as in the days of old.
Remember me for good to the master you have,
I was wronged and ended in this place you deplored.

He forgot, and that is how it was meant to be
For God determined when Joseph should be made free:
It was till two years hence when Pharaoh dreamt a dream
And he was made second in Egypt by degree.

DEATHBED

They gathered round her and were very sad,
Watching with their eyes her weak fading breath,
Stretched on a soft bed she was not unclad,
Lying down she walked to the door of death.

Family and friends were with her that day
As she lay dying on her clean deathbed,
Knowing that quite soon she will go away
Out of this life to the land of the dead.

Lord Jesus while ill clad, nailed to a wood
Saw His mother and disciple quite near
And a vast crowd that shouted where they stood
With priests and scribes, happy to mock and jeer.

They sneered the Almighty whose life He gave,
The world's Creator, eternal Logos
Who loved His own and whom He came to save
With pain on His deathbed, a wooden cross.

RAHAB

"Now therefore, I pray you, swear unto me by the Lord, since I have showed you kindness, that you will also show kindness unto my father's house, and give me a token" (Joshua 2:12).

A young woman of ill repute
Lived in the town of Jericho,
Worshipped idols, a prostitute
Who of God's might she learnt to know.

She heard how God with His great might
 Released the slaves and set them free,
Killed Egypt's firstborn in the night
And then drowned Pharaoh in the sea.

For the children of Israel
Made to their God an urgent plea,
He saved them by plagues that were real
And drowned Pharaoh's host in the sea.

They marched to the land of Canaan,
After they crossed the sea dry shod
Conquered kings as does a Sultan:
The Lord Jehovah was their God.

They sent spies to see the layout
 Of Jericho for their attack;
Of their conquest there was no doubt
With God's power aiding their back.

The townsfolk saw them and they fled
And went to Rahab's house to hide;
She told the chasers that they sped
Into the wilderness outside.

Your God is a most mighty Lord,
Our dread of Him made our hearts melt,
You have slain us as will your sword,
No words can tell the fear we felt.

Rahab asked that they will let live
Herself and family, in time
When their great God will move to give
To them the land for all its crimes.

Put a red thread in the window
It will let all our people see
And preserve you from all the woe:
Our oath will keep your people free.

Rahab, the harlot, and her kin
Lived with God's people all her life,
Was ancestor to Christ the king
For to Salmon she was a wife.

THE UNBELIEVER

"For the invisible things of him from the creation of the world are clearly seen, being understood by the things that are made" (Romans 1:20)

How foolish you will appear
Before the Lord, the Judge;
You railed Him when on earth
And His presence begrudged.
You smote Him with your hands
And scourged and crucified
And spat on Him and cursed
And mocked and vilified.

How foolish you will appear
Before the Lord, the Judge
When you spent your whole life
With nature that did not nudge
Your conscience to perceive
A Creator and believe,
But persisted to teach
Evolution in your speech.

How foolish you will appear
When you explored the heavens,
The planets and the stars,
And great galaxies afar
And nebulae and wonders,
But you did not ponder
That God created all;
How great will be your fall!

It will then be too late
For you to change your mind
Or to say you were wrong,
For God, merciful and kind,
Will not give a second chance
For you to correct your wrong;
Wail, wail, your doom is great,
No escape, it is too late.

ON THE SEA SHORE

"But when the morning was now come, Jesus stood on the shore: but the disciples knew not that it was Jesus" (John 21:4).

On the shore stood Jesus and said,
Children, have you caught any meat?
For they cast their nets and spread
And did not catch a fish to eat.

They were fishing throughout the night
And laboured hard without reward
Then Jesus called, throw to the right,
He knew for he was Christ the Lord.

It is the Lord, John said aloud,
Peter covered himself and ran
For previously he had avowed
That he did not know Christ, the man.

They dragged the net with much struggle
For it was laden with great fish,
Did not tear despite the hassle:
There was meat for many a dish.

They saw the Lord with a coal fire
With fish and bread for them to eat;
They knew Him and did not enquire
Who was this man that they did meet.

He said, Peter, do you love Me?
He answered, you know Lord I do;
He asked him not one time, but three
And said, feed my lambs and sheep too.

This, the third time to them appeared
Jesus who rose up from the dead;
Restored Peter who was endeared
That, through him, all His sheep are fed.

THE FALL

"And they heard the voice of the Lord God walking in the garden in the cool of the day" (Genesis 3:8).

God came down at the break of day
To deal with man who went astray,
Whose state of blessedness was gone
When his rebellious deed was done
When Adam and Eve failed to shun
Satan who filled their heart of clay.

The curse of justice quickly fell
Upon mankind, now ripe for hell
Except for One, the woman's seed
Who by His life and noble deed
Crushed the devil and saved indeed
Captive sinners in Satan's spell.

He smote the devil's haughty head
By dying freely in man's stead;
He suffered by His Father's hand
For He alone was strong to stand;
There was none other in the land
To die and rise up from the dead.

A FALLEN WORLD

"By one man sin entered into the world, and death by sin"
(Romans 5:12).

We have traversed the burning galaxies, my friend
And have at last arrived at our journey's end.

Hidden behind the face of a middle-aged sun
In constant third orbit, Earth will persist to run
Till one day it rises to ring salvation's bell
Or else be hurled to burn through the porches of Hell.
Let us now examine the living world and see
The nature of its life, and fathom what might be.

What transcendent beauty adorns the high terrain
Where mountains touch the clouds above the fertile plain!
An eagle lifts a hare with deadly sabre claws
And tears it with its beak, strong as the tiger's jaws.
A life is slain so that the eagle's young may live:
The poor furry creature was unwilling to give
Its flesh for another, to be eaten alive:
Vainly did it struggle and vainly did it strive!
Further down the mountain there lies a bright red stain
Of a ravaged grazing lamb that the wolf had slain.
Oh, what raging violence! Let us go elsewhere
Till we discover hope beyond this dark nightmare.

Rumbling guts belch out fire from a volcano's mouth
In the hard frozen north and the temperate south;
Earth's shoulders are shaking, as if rising from sleep
While ocean beds collide with each other and creep

Bringing havoc and fury that destroy and maul
Creatures buried in dark pits as soon as they fall.
Disaster upon disaster: death's fangs are unfurled,
Jaws and beaks drip with blood, agony fills the world.

The Earth's mighty oceans, many a trackless sea
Contain vigorous life, seemingly free,
But in the deep waters the strong devour the weak
While the howling whirlwind nudges the island's peak;
Who can stay its power? It fiercely comes this way:
Churns the wind of heaven as darkness rules the day,
Yet the valiant human attempts to ride the storm:
Is his life a struggle, calamity the norm?
Let us hurry skyward until the storm is spent,
Then return to find out if he is straight or bent.

He stands upright, not crawling upon foot or hand,
Unlike creatures looking down when they fly or stand,
He, with skilful hands, forms his own creation,
Child of a fertile brain which rejects frustration.
We escaped his rocket reaching the outer sky,
A mark of his genius that never fails to try.
He traverses the Earth in his flying machines,
Sails the sea, digs the land, and conquers the deep ravines;
Let us observe if life has smiled on him or frowned
For upon the planet no equal can be found.

Hear her cry of lament: her stillborn is well formed,
Hear her weep in the night: her baby is deformed;
That bereft mother wails: within her womb he died,
His life could not return however much she cried.
Watch him in the prime of youth, stricken by disease,
Breath hanging on a string with no comfort or ease:
Pain strikes the nerve endings as lightning strikes the skies,
The soul is crushed, tears fail to solace when it cries.
The old man, confined to bed, cannot rise and walk

Nor attend to himself, with face as white as chalk;
The woman in the street, with stick and shabby dress,
Falls victim to a car, becomes a black red mess.
Man's days seem insubstantial, as dust in the pan,
Death waits outside his house to shorten his life span,
At times it is demure, and knocks his wooden door,
At times, with violence, slays him upon the floor;
Few are strong to face it, most men will weep and cry,
Knowing its certain demand, yet they fear to die;
Man is one by nature, all men are born to die,
All men are bon to suffer, all men are born to cry.

See what splendid honour man shows in every way
While he suffers hardship and seeks those gone astray;
He bears pain and hunger to feed his little ones,
Defies untold danger, the muzzles of the guns.
He climbs up the rock face to save one trapped alone,
Knowing a fall will cause the breaking of each bone.
Even in the ocean he takes the stranger's side
Though the sharks may slay him, the fury of the tide.
Life hangs in the balance, he struggles for his kin,
Health may fail, advancing age creases up his skin.
Man is a great wonder, most noble, true and wise,
Who would wish him evil or witness his demise?
Look, he charged the lion so that his child may run,
He is mauled and dying in the harsh blazing sun.

What are those clouds, hovering thick and black,
Unlike the clouds of heaven, no lustre on their back?
They are the signs of tumult, of men engaged in war
Where the rockets shatter the living by the score.
Thousands of explosives litter the burning sky,
Fall upon cities, thousands of people die
While in alleys and houses, slaughter and rape are done,
Bellies opened, heads smashed, no one escapes, not one.
Is this an exception that man performs such deeds?

Have we not seen him suffer for his fellow's needs?
Let us search the whole earth for the subtle answer,
A play cannot be judged by a single dancer.

In cities, in jungles, the story is the same,
Culture lends him no escape from this evil game.
Man cannot rid himself of what he is inside,
His venom is cast out with defiance and pride.
He boasts of hurtful deeds, rewards his fighting men,
Leaves the weak and poor like a disembowelled hen;
Look upon his actions, he is worse than the beast:
It kills to feed hunger, but he to gloat and feast;
Master of the Earth, he keeps creatures in his grasp,
But in his heart there lies the poison of the asp.
He could not conquer greed nor lust and love of fame
Nor overcome his desire to build himself a name.

Look at that young woman, she gave body and mind
While he seeks another, and another to find,
Casts his children away to dire hardship and need,
To gratify his lust, he spits upon his seed.
One, for love of money, betrays his closest trust,
Plotting with skill and craft to place men in the dust.
Mass murder is performed on progeny unborn
Where in their mothers' wombs they are destroyed and torn.
Yes, his moral nature is lesser than the brute:
He uproots his own kind and of the womb the fruit.
Man stood upon the moon and sent spaceships above,
Yet cannot live on Earth and show sufficient love.
Let us investigate if this has always been
And look into his past to see what could be seen.

Structures of past ages are scattered in the lands
On the mountains and greens and in desert sands;
Skyscrapers nudge the sky in a proud upward drift,
Like ancient monuments show a genius's gift,

But the tale is of war, of bloodshed from times past,
Of conquerors and slaves, of glory running fast,
Of tales of one who wept when naught was left to spoil,
While the blood of innocents drowned the thirsty soil.
Though man's learning has increased, within his heart is found
Spreading roots of enmity, cruelty unbound.
Man is a paradox, possessing good and ill,
His reason and desires support a wayward will,
Meets death for another, yet another betrays,
Strives that life be preserved and then butchers and slays.
The fury of nature lasts for a brief moment,
Calm follows howling storms, but man creates torment,
Millions fell to his bombs, to his sword and rockets,
Heads fell down, throats were cut, eyes removed from sockets,
But the seas and mountain, the free wind of the storm
Raged to claim a thousand of life of every form.

Like a lost ship adrift, far from the peaceful dock
Life is steered by evil against a mighty rock
And in the deepest darkness the soul of man will grope
Till he walks in God's way, his only certain hope.

Did the wise Creator make this planet to be
A home for snakes and scorpions and deadly enmity?
Violence rules creatures, the entire life-filled world:
The Earth has earned Hades, therein it may be hurled.
Come to the beginning, search what the Lord has made
Ere the day when Adam betrayed his God and strayed.

He walked with his Maker in a garden of trees,
Of beauty and riches, made to nourish and please;
Clad with splendid features and fine moral stature,
Was made warden of Earth, of its ordered nature.
When the Devil tricked him, disaster struck them all,
The ancient Book recalls what man now calls the Fall.

Death and ill stormed the world and became his lot,
Corruption in his frame, sin on his soul a blot.
Man, like his monuments, shows relics of his past
When he walked with God and kept his goodness fast.

Here, there in the darkness shines a flickering light:
Men are born of God's life and rescued from the night.
Yes, a great mystery took place upon this Earth
When our Lord, most humbly received His human birth.
We look with wide wonder upon this stretch of soil
To see where man's Saviour, with His blood did foil
The work of the Evil One so that one day the morn
Of a new world and Earth will be truly reborn.

Let us return swiftly through the fulness of space
And report that evil is rampant in this place,
See in our Maker's hands His scars of matchless grace.

THE HURRICANE

Roll and toss, O waves of the sea,
Cover the bondslave, drown the free,
Leap like catfish into the air,
Challenge the dragon in its lair;
Twist and turn, ye wind of the sky
Bring down the cables raised up high,
Uproot each building and tall tree,
Lift a bus as you lift a flea.
Rage, oh rage, ye heavens and earth,
Stir the foundations of your birth,
Come from the womb, behold the land,
Filled with men as ants on the sand.
Roll, roll, the billows of the sea,
Cause men to die, fish to be free;
Advance a wall of warring shields,
Sound the charge and cover the fields.

Palm tree of graceful stately height,
Can you withstand the wind? Its might?
When caressed by its gentle hand,
You waved with dancing to its band;
Sway not your head, but hang it down,
Else you will lose your neck and crown:
The hurricane races your way,
Prepared to overwhelm the day;
Look not upon it lest you die,
Turn your eyes from the cyclops' eye.

Destruction is left in its trail:
Earth is struck by a comet's tail,
Leaving life dying in its wake,

Sparing the fish and water snake;
Man's strong buildings crumbled and fell,
Were carried by the rising swell,
Float wood of homes, chattels of glass:
Scattered debris on watery grass;
Men, shut your ears, the children cry
As they are washed away and die;
They fell helpless to wind and wave
Which charged the wood, the mountain cave;
The fierce hurricane passed along,
Weak men trembled, as did the strong.

THE RAPE OF KUWAIT AUGUST 1990

Great tanks came rolling down the street,
The chains crackled, the road buckled,
Men fell like harvest grains of wheat;
Infants and babies who suckled
Were blown till they were chunks of meat;
Men and women killed or shackled
Were harassed by the armoured fleet
While young soldiers laughed and chuckled
Treading them down with their strong feet.

High heaven heard and sorely wept,
Shedding its tears, black as the night;
A woman wailed her son who slept
The sleep of death before her sight
Beneath the spreading jet-black cloud
Of smoke-filled sky, the burning suns
Of oil wells in the land once proud
Where men have fallen to the guns,
Where slaughter, robbery were fun,
Possessions carried by the ton.
The wealthy peaceful Gulf that gave
Fish in abundance, weeds and oil
Was turned into an open grave
Of birds and fish held in its soil.
Once seamen sailed the waves of light,
Made viscid with petroleum, black,
Where open sea and shoreline bight
Were filled with dead creatures and wrack.

Corruption in the earth was done
While flames threatened to burn the sky;
Rare darkness overwhelmed the sun
Were men were seized and held to die.
The helpless in their motherland
Perished by the assassin's hand.

MANKIND

"For all have sinned, and come short of the glory of God"
(Romans 3:23)

It was as if a dream had passed
Before my wondering face,
As if my mind had floated out
Into the darkness of space
Yet could look down, view and survey
The steps of the human race,
Mind its present and see its past
In one unbroken embrace.
As if the passing of the years
Regressed in a slothful pace.

It looked as if nature was pure
Innocent, fragrant and bright,
As if mankind raped its honour
With violence and with might;
Moral darkness covered the land
That once upheld man's right
That once followed the way of God
Rejecting the deeds of night;
Men were locked in a fatal clasp
In a most terrible fight
Trying to shed their fellow's blood
As if they possessed the right.

Once he killed with a wooden club
Then with spear, with sword and knife;

Now he adds great rockets and guns
To destroy his brother's life
And in the darkness of the night
He steals another man's wife
As if he is driven by lust,
By wanton hatred and strife.

I looked and saw upon the street
A lady with no foothold:
She had slipped upon the pavement
Whose frozen surface was cold;
Men and women rushed to her aid
To raise her up and uphold,
To lift the fallen or broken,
To strengthen a heart once bold.
I saw some value human life
More than silver and gold,
Would offer their life a ransom
For a loved one, weak and old.

Yet upon the neighbouring street
A handbag is snatched away:
A woman is thrown to the ground
To become a mugger's prey.
Some fear to settle in their homes
Whether by night or by day,
Dreading that they may be attacked
By burglars who maim and slay.
I saw the poor starving for food
While rich men throw it away
And men owning other men's lives
Who beg for mercy and pray
Falling humbled in filth and dust
While violent masters bray.

Should evil or accident strike
Men rush eagerly to save,
To give solace and help to those
Unable for help to crave,
Yet nations mass out great armies
To send to a bloody grave
Thousands upon thousands of men:
Young soldiers, loyal and brave;
The bombs are thrown, people are blown,
Tall buildings crumble and cave
On all manner of men and beasts,
Not sparing the lord or knave.

How can honour and sacrifice,
Love and compassion combine
With hatred, greed and enmity
In the noble human line?
I thought there must be an answer
To unfold, expose, define
Man's notions for such behaviour
Which he falters to outline,
Then I discovered the Bible
Whose message was true, divine.

It told how the Lord Almighty
Created from simple clay
Our father, from whom our mother
Sprang into the new world's ray;
Of all the trees of Paradise
One was forbidden that day:
A simple test of obedience
That fealty may hold its sway,
But they determined to rebuff,
Transgress, rebel and betray.

Death marched on a cursed universe
Till all creatures were ensnared,
None could flee its hideous power
However he tried or dared,
Evil reigned in the soul of man:
At first it pondered and stared.
Man strikes down his harmless neighbour
Yet pities a wounded bird;
Of all creatures of the world
His fellow renders him scared,
He fails to acknowledge evil
Though at his own soul he glared
Yet God offers new life through faith
For He is a God who cared.

INVASION OF KUWAIT AUGUST 1990

Father,
Did you hear the engines roaring?
Did you see the soldier's pouring?
And the noisy rockets soaring
Down the street, past your feet?

Did you feel the earth was shaking?
Did you think the ground was breaking?
Did you hear the dead bones quaking
As if being reclothed with meat?

Did you see the oil wells burning?
Blue waters to blackness turning
And the deep sea billows churning
The slurping oil slick passing by?

Did you see the seagulls drowning?
Cormorant and white tern browning
And gigantic thick fumes crowning
The land and covering the sky?

Did you hear the great guns speaking?
Dusty chained metal wheels squeaking?
Did you see water drums leaking
And fighter planes screaming on high?

Were your dry bones ready, restless

As men's proud heads fell down senseless?
Father, you have heard the helpless,
Wait until the last trumpet's cry.

It is the time of oppression,
For men to practise transgression,
To take another's possession,
It is not Resurrection Day.

The neighbour, with rude obsession,
Proclaimed God in his confession,
Then invaded with aggression
To ravage, rape and to inveigh.

The tanks rolled in, the guns were manned,
Destruction reigned, almost offhand,
No one was able to withstand
Those who entered to rob and slay.

There, in the heart of the city,
Mercy perished, as did pity,
Squashed by boots, studded and gritty
Where carefree children used to play.

Your wife, a widow, was ailing
As her health and strength were failing
While the soldiers were assailing
The homes of their innocent prey.

She should be with you when she dies,
When death comes in to close her eyes,
Her place stays vacant till you rise,:
She will sleep in a different clay.

Friends moved her to a new domain

While daily, fresh blood from the slain,
Drenched the soldiers who killed like Cain
Too weak to plead, she went away.

They left you in the ground alone
Lying beneath a marble stone
Which truly is a safer zone
Until the Resurrection Day.

AFRICA

Those walking skeletons covered with skin,
Exposed in all parts with sores on the shin
Are too young for hair o grow on the chin,
Too lean for death: it snatches hundreds in.

Squatting skeletons upon the dry ground,
Motionless and silent without a sound,
Oblivious that burial pits are found,
Cluttered with corpses till their turn comes round.

Exhausted skeletons show no surprise
When their mouths and noses are covered with flies
That suck the moisture from these and their eyes
As they lay helpless unable to rise.

We watch them on the television screen
Between food adverts, which seem obscene,
With no other record that they have been
A part of this world, struck in a latrine.

The nations supplied food and drugs to heal,
But bellies swelled for the lack of a meal
When warring scoundrels continued to steal
And mercy died in hearts moulded of steel.

O Lord, speed the time when justice prevails
That food may reach camps, villages and vales,
The land of the vacant mouth and entrails
Where the weak cannot cry when death assails.

MAN'S WILL

"For out of the heart proceed evil thoughts, murders, adulteries, fornications, thefts, false witness, blasphemies"
(Matthew 15:19).

They say that man is free to choose,
To gain his life or perhaps lose,
But in his heart there burns a fire
Of lust and of wayward desire.
All things seem subject to his will,
He summons death to slay and kill,
To execute his fellow man
With a skilful and deadly plan.

Who is not stained by thoughts of wrong
To crush the weak and praise the strong?
To lust after his neighbour's wife?
Threaten their peace, and secure life?
Yes, men are bound by what they are
As in its course each distant star,
Their carnal hearts master their will
To bring forth hideous deeds of ill.

Can freedom reach a soul enchained
By its own lust or treasure gained?

Or is it buried in the mire,
Slain by the arrows of desire?
Freedom is born through sacrifice
Through the Lord's blood which did suffice
To cleanse the heart of ill and shame
By simple faith in His great name.

THERE IS NONE RIGHTEOUS

"There is none righteous, no, not one" (Romans 3:10).

Who can stand before his Maker and boldly confess,
My deeds have been righteous, Heaven is mine to possess?
When the mighty Creator is purer than the light
And the purest deeds of men are darker than the night?

Who can stand and dare to say, my thoughts are ever clean?
My mind has never transgressed, nor thought of the obscene?
When the Lord of Heaven looks down on the heart and sees
That sin has filled man's soul as fishes fill the seas?

Who can ask with honesty, which of God's laws I broke?
Man is like an eastern ox, is burdened with a yoke,
The yoke of his sinful heart which cannot truly say,
I have lived to God's glory each second of each day.

Man tries to reach God's standard, but all his efforts fail:
God came to earth through Jesus to conquer and prevail,
To provide Christ's righteousness, the Saviour of mankind,
As the robe for sinful men who trust the One most kind.

PROVIDENCE

Man's glory is like a flower:
Here today and tomorrow gone
But the Lord's word and His power
Remain more steadfast than the sun.

High in the sky, racing lower
The disc of light, its course begun,
Ushers the night with clouds of fire:
His word commands the setting sun.

His truth grows sweeter every hour;
His word, like stallions in full run
Mightier than death, dreadful and sour,
Gives radiance to the rising sun.

Harvester of seed and sower:
The heart is where His work is done;
Yielding fruit in drought of summer:
His word brings hope in Christ the Son.

O Word of God, You are my tower;
I hide in You, O holy One;
Let Your Spirit's mighty shower
Fall upon me O God the Son.

BONDAGE

"Know ye not, that to whom ye yield yourselves servants to obey, his servants ye are to whom ye obey; whether of sin unto death, or obedience unto righteousness?" (Romans 6:16)

A man may seem upright, yet his own heart betrays
The lust pangs of his soul, the secret of his ways
That ride upon his back like lofty maidens, proud,
Urging his will to crawl until his neck is bowed.

Great forces drive the soul to do a shameful act
When it knows it is wrong and yet cannot retract
Then weeps with deep regret until next time comes round
To struggle and to fall upon the stony ground.

But there is strength in God to battle and endure
The darts of evil thoughts until the heart is pure,
Until temptations flee, hard driven by our blows,
Until we learn to trust the Lord in all our woes.

ADVENT

"Then said I, Lo, I come (in the volume of the book it is written of me), to do thy will, O God" (Hebrews 10:7)

Hear, O Lands, the amazing news,
Come, O People, reflect and muse:
God in the womb entered a shed,
Was born in poverty and dread.

Obedient to His Father's will
The Son of Man remained God still;
While people slept in their homestead
He had no place to lay His head.

He wrought salvation with His arm
And ransomed men from hell and harm;
His blood was shed upon the cross,
All else in life is show and dross.

BETHLEHEM

"There was no room for them in the inn" (Luke 2:7).

The inn is too crowded, the night is enshrouded
By a mantle of deep black;
I think I can help you, may Heaven defend you
Oh, how can I turn you back?
Please go to the stable, your donkey is able
To feed on the straw and hay
And there with God's creatures of familiar features
Shelter through the night and day.

God has prepared our way, opened the path today,
Come Miriam, heavy with child;
Come, rest beneath the roof, not in the field aloof
Where ravenous beasts run wild;
Far from the noise of men, the tumult of the den
Your travail will not be heard,
The cattle will stand by and will not mind your cry
Nor will they fret or be scared.

Through God's mercy indeed, the governor decreed
To usher salvation's morn.
The prophets long foretold: in Bethlehem of old
The Redeemer will be born.
Our Lord rules over all, the heathen heed His call
And act His story so well.
The creation did long for one who be strong
To deliver it from hell.

REPENTANCE

Weary my soul, my mind, my heart
I lay on You my sadness,
Refresh me like a newborn hart
That leaps with joy and gladness.

My soul is laden like a cart:
A bridled mule in harness;
Come to my aid, give me a start
Out of the mire and darkness.

Hell bound by sin, yet torn apart,
I cry in pain and weakness;
Come, cleanse my soul in every part
To taste of grace the sweetness.

Forget the sins of my dark past:
In Christ I plead forgiveness;
Make me Your own while life shall last
To live and praise Your greatness.

LIKE SEAGULLS

Lord of heaven and earth and see,
Hear my fervent prayer and plea,
Remember my loved ones, remember me,
Please help the needy refugee.

Scattered like seagulls upon the sand
Far from our home and motherland,
Let us each one persist to stand
With grace and favour from Your hand.

With lonely hearts we face the day
Bowed as the wind on standing hay;
O God, our only strength and stay
Keep us secure, turn not away.

Open our eyes that we may see
The Lamb of God upon the tree;
Save us from bondage, set us free:
Our praise shall rise eternally.

THE ATHEIST'S FAITH

Let me tell you what happened, the atheist said,
A very long time ago when your god was dead,
And in passing, let me say, he is dead today
For he never existed, never had a say.

By chance there was a mass of microscopic size
From which all known elements were to form and rise,
A dense mass of hydrogen, basis of all things,
Of minerals, gases, and life on feet and wings.
Let me interrupt, I said, do you really mean
That the weight of billions of stars could thus have been
Entrapped within a ball that could fit my hand,
The galaxies, the planets, moons and seas and land?
Yes, he said a gaseous mass from which all things came:
Stormy skies, and living things which possess a name,
The spinning galaxies and nebulae out there,
All that is in space, yes, everything, everywhere,
Mind you, I do not know how this ball came to be
But that it was there, all good scientists agree.
There was a great explosion, now called the Big Bang
And the gases were scattered faster than any mustang
The expanding universe proves the great event
Ten billion years ago, and its force is not spent
For it still expands today, fuelled with great might:
The big Bang and not your god created the light.
No one was there to observe how it came about
But for the fact it happened there could be no doubt.

I said, you now tell me a preposterous tale
That the mass of all matter could fit in a pail,
The weight of the universe in a single ball
That was of such a size that could be graded small.

Indeed, let me tell you, this is how it began,
The gases gathered to form the children of Pan
Which all rotated around till some great chunk escaped
To form distant stars from which planets were shaped.
Our Earth was such a lump that drifted from the sun
And then it cooled down as it rotated and spun.
With the passage of time some slimy mass appeared
And then life began as the molecules adhered
Each to the other forming chains, the essence of life
From their various acids which at that time was rife.
One celled organisms divided to complex forms
Which were duly adapted to all kinds of storms
Until, with the passage of millions of earth years,
Complex life diversified in both hemispheres
Some think that life on earth started in outer space
Hitchhiking on a comet, landed in some place.

Just a minute, I said, what a fantastic tale:
An exploding fireball forms butterfly and snail
And thousands of species of insects, birds and trees,
Dinosaurs and sharks, frogs and eagles, man and fleas,
An expanding gaseous ball, given enough time
Forms a fragrant English rose and the mountain thyme
Robin red-breast, bumble bee, lavender and lime,
Biochemical cycles, many an enzyme.
We do not fully know the functions of the cell
Nor what life really is, yet you venture to tell
That some luck and chance produced all that exists

And this process still goes on, it grows and persists.
Go, tell it to the marines, it is a great lie
And no greater can be found underneath the sky.
You indeed are a man of faith, hence you advance
Fantasies against common sense built upon chance.
 I believe that my God created all of this:
The heavens and earth and all that in them is.

NO BEAUTY OIL

Man's esteemed life, ensnared in sin,
Cannot reverse the curse within,
It falls to cancer and disease
Like rotting apples on the trees.

Should life be long, his skin will crease
Till he fulfils his rented lease;
His bones and joints may with pain
Or stroke destroys half of his brain.

No beauty oil or cleansing cream
Can hide her wrinkles when they scream,
The tints and colours of her hair
Are camouflage for what is there,

No medicine or purchased care
Halts the process of wear and tear,
The rich, the wise, like fools may drool,
Disintegrate like skunk or mule.

All those in whose lives Christ did reign
Will rise to be renewed again,
But the rebellious will be spewed
Into hell's torment, unsubdued.

FOLLY

How does new life shoot from the dust
Where dead bones lie with wood and rust,
Nauseating stench beneath the crust?
There, time abandoned hope and trust,
Desire is dead, as honour, lust,
Weak men, untrue and others just
Decomposing most hideously.

The tiny seed will grow to make
A large tree when its shell will break,
Cleaving the earth when Spring does wake.
It forms the wood for bed and stake,
For fire to burn and sparks to flake,
The soil becomes these wondrously.

From seed too small for eyes to see
Comes a child from the inner sea
Crying for breath on mother's knee,
More helpless than the calf is he
Yet stronger than the ox will be,
Is part of nature, part of me
And part of mankind truthfully.

Watch how the grains of Summer's wheat
Will turn to bread sold on the street,
Likewise, the babe must grow and eat:
Milk turns to skin and bones and meat,
To growing brains and growing feet,
To flesh and blood most readily.

Thus, from elements, mean and weak,
A man is formed to cry and speak
With tongue, fierce as the eagle's beak.
Riches are his to search and seek,
He stands upon his ego's peak,
Defies the proud, abhors the meek,
Despises all men haughtily.

Where creatures of the soil are found,
His body shall be boxed or bound
And left six feet within the ground.
Silent and still, without a sound,
Rotting beneath a raised up mound.
The graves are full, the dead abound,
They had to go unwillingly.

And does not Folly utter lies
That when death comes to close men's eyes,
Each one like meaner creature dies
Without punishment, without prize?
Its children think that they are wise:
The fool looks for shadows and sighs
When none shall live eternally.

Men scoff at God with their replies,
Yet they shall find to their surprise
That they, like all the dead, shall rise
To stand before the One all wise
And answer for their guilt and lies.
Lord, must I hear their wildest cries
When they perish eternally?

PRIDE

"A man's pride shall bring him low" (Proverbs 29:23).

Clay upon hardened clay has walked,
Opened wide his mouth and talked,
A stench escaped from a jar uncorked.

He talked as if he would never die,
His tongue defied the earth and sky,
But his clay within the clay shall lie.

All life is mine, he proudly said,
The living now as were the dead,
Yet he cannot sow hair on his head.

He did not earn his looks or mind:
Gifts come from God for He is kind
 And showers His blessings upon mankind.

Self-esteem blinds his mind and will,
Each day he grows haughtier still,
But a virus can seize him and kill.

His vain body may dance and sway,
A clot of blood his heart can slay
For worms to consume him in the clay.

As a lion outside the den
He lives his three score and ten,
Like beasts shall perish, not knowing when.

He forgets God and does not think
That in death's lap his life shall sink
Until the grave vomits out his stink.

Many a beauty once had been
That wizened when death's face was seen,
Eyes closed in darkness that once were keen.

Riches halt not the stride of time,
He shall lay in the clay and lime
Without a penny, without a dime.

O lump of clay, arrogant, loud,
Before your birth time kept your shroud,
The wriggling worms shall feed on the pride.

AT TWILIGHT

When night descends upon city and field
My eyelids close melodiously to yield
To the arms of sleep, caressed by its hand
As darkness robes the splendour of the land,
Then in my twilight moments I recall
The scenes of life, the triumph and the fall,
The powerful who live a life most fair,
The miserable, in fear and despair,
The poor disgraced before men's cruel eyes,
The proud thriving on treachery and lies.

I recall the meek, tossed like tennis balls,
Unjustly confined within prison walls,
The rowdy free, unmoved by ill or word,
Held by sensuous smiles, by whispers heard.
The old, on the whole, are not full of days,
The young may not see the end of their ways:
The pitfalls abound for the youthful feet
Who presume to face all the traps they meet
Along the paths that lead to drugs and pain,
To death which waits within alley and lane
Until their soul is like a finger, lost
In heat of battle or Antarctic frost.
When the sun rises to deport the night
They cannot abide the pure morning light
But lie in dungeons where darkness prevails
Far from the mountains, the green field and dales.

I clearly see that life's journey is short
Though most will refuse to leave it and will snort
When their hour draws near to the hungry grave:
The cowards are many, few are the brave.

There is beyond time a Heaven made sure
For all who honour God, the blessed poor,
But a place remains, dreadful to behold
For those who remain in the devil's hold.

THE OPPRESSED

Oh, bitterness, is there no end?
Will heaven cleave, mercy descend?
The body withers with the soul
While tyrants kick them like a ball.

Rising a while, again to fall,
Danger without, within the gall,
Only their death will satisfy
Disdainful men deaf to their cry.

And some remain, they shall not die
Though raging men and hell reply;
The seed, though crushed, will grow again
Until new life will fill the plain.

The summer heat, the winter rain
Will bless the furrow bearing grain;
When seasons have tarried and run
The stem will shoot towards the sun.

The tempest raged, then it was gone:
Men and houses fell as one;
The newborn crying out of sight
Carries the nation's life tonight.

FREEDOM

Look how he creeps on hands and knees
Pulling hard at the binding straps,
An infant knows not what he sees
Will free himself from bonds that trap.

It hatches in the nest and sings,
Is kept from the predator's mouth.
The fledgling learns to beat its wings:
Propellers that will take it south.

Floating across the dark grey sky
The cloud bestows water and shade,
Moving towards where eagles fly
Freely across valley and glade.

Creatures reject bondage, capture,
Insects and fish, mammals and birds,
Freedom is their right by nature,
The prairie fox, the cattle herds.

God's gift given to all mankind
Yet not enjoyed by all who can;
Some are compelled to dig and grind
While kept in chains by fellow man.

Why are the thousands held in cages
Forbidden the green hills and sea?
Despair rules, the mind engages
Hope that they one day be free.

The baby breaths free air at birth,
Shares the freedom for which men crave
While evil villains of the earth
Enslave the weak until the grave.

Rise, living flame within the poor
Buffeted on the rocks and stones,
No mortal can kill or obscure
Your fire within your children's bones.

Dying today, born tomorrow
Hanged unjustly and bound in shame
Yet from the graveyard of sorrow
Your sons will rise to bear your name.

Desire of all, owned by the few,
You heed the cries of those who call,
Oppressors never though or knew
That your sons will secure their fall.

Some lived in dungeons of the night,
Some had to run to save their skin,
But will stand strong to gain their right
And prove that courage is their twin.

THE VILLAGE CHURCH

Kneel my soul before the service starts,
There is time to remember
The common fire in our souls and hearts
That left a single ember.

One large family in bygone days,
We went to church together
And raised our voices in hymns of praise
In fair and stormy weather.

Our parents joined the singing aloud,
Though small, we tried to follow,
Were told that we should never be proud
Nor should our hearts be hollow.

As children we rushed to Sunday School,
To hear of Jesus the Lord;
We leant of the wise man and the fool,
Had no reason to be bored.

My father called us daily to pray
While falling on our knees,
But Sunday was a most holy day
As the bell rang through the trees.

Lonely church, wounded by time that stands
Amidst the elm trees and oak
Which scattered sunlight that fell in bands
On Reverend Morgan's cloak.

It metallic spire with sabre point
Reached upwards toward the sky
To lift our eyes to Heaven and point
To our blessed home on high.

O quiet Graveyard, with grey on green,
How sadly I often stood
Where primroses, daffodils were seen
And the cuckoos chimed in the wood.

When small I wondered how bodies slept
In the restful arms of death,
Their spirits gone to God to be kept,
Transported by their last breath.

Within the church my sister married
The man she loved so well
 And in the grave we came and buried
Her frame that in childbirth fell.

Her wedding bells that shattered the air
Then rang their mournful slow knell;
How I miss you my sister, most fair,
Much more than verses can tell.

My elder brother ventured to make
A living in the city,
But he did not utterly forsake
The home of love and pity.

Where compassion manifestly showed
In fire, teapot and kettle,
Where God's love made our home its abode
In grounds with sheep and cattle.

Dare I remember them and not weep
For parents, sister, brother?
For my sister in death's long sleep
Who fell amidst the heather.

Their bodies are there, their souls are found
Resting in our Defender;
I love that parcel of sacred ground,
My bed when I surrender.

DEATH OF A CHRISTIAN LADY

"Blessed are the dead which die in the Lord"
(Revelation 14:13)

Death came to share a woman's bed,
He was dismayed he caused no dread
When his proud chest and hands were red
With blood from those who ran and fled.
Though cancer grew in her and spread
Death was her slave, it will be said
For he could see his pathway led
To Heaven, to Christ, her living head:
Death wails that glory lies ahead.

He saw her then began to snore,
Weary of plucking field and shore.
He will leave her a few days more,
She might beg him upon the floor,
For he regards himself at war
With her spirit, until his roar
Will frighten her soul to its core.
Till the he had a plan in store:
To knock hard at the neighbour's door.

Many people, in such a state
Will accuse God and curse and hate.
It is the lot of man, his fate
To meet his death, however late.
The grave consumes humans like bait,
Its hunger grows, will not abate,

It cries when men enter its gate
Through murder, war, or simple freight,
Bring more, bring more, I hardly ate.

With weakened body and thin hair,
She will fall into death's dark lair
To be a part of what men share,
But in the twilight she could bear
And knew that she will surely stare
On Him who wrapped her in His care;
Her body will rise from the snare
When Jesus comes back in the air
To tell the dead: rise up and stir.

Though nearing the end of her race,
She wanted news of God's good grace,
Of those who once lived in disgrace
And now are found in Christ's embrace.
Since Christ has died, no man is base,
No virtue gained through birth or race,
Each must mind God and seek His face.
Should death speed up his slothful pace,
Heaven will be her resting place.

Her friends sang hymns, Scripture was read,
They praised the Christ who died and bled
Whose life was offered in their stead,
 Death shall in hell ruffle his bed;
For them there is new life instead
And resurrection time ahead.
But they missed her and tears were shed
And in deep sorrow bowed the head,
Showed how Christians bury their dead.

DEATH IS SWALLOWED UP IN VICTORY

"That through death he might destroy him that had the power of death, that is, the devil" (Hebrews 2:14).

A short period, soon after the birth of time,
The first man stood upon the earth, sublime,
The pinnacle of all created life
With a free will to choose, to fall or climb.

The tempter came in a serpent's guise
With a vain promise of a precious prize,
The prize of knowledge of all good and ill
Whereby man would become knowing and wise.

The hissing serpent drew closer to Eve,
Armed with evil lies to make her believe
That they could become as wise as their God:
Such was his subtle method to deceive.

He slandered God and said that He was mean
And that His command was truly obscene,
His threats were empty and would never stand
When wisdom was waiting for them to glean.

He said, it is not true that you will die
As Death waited tensely for her reply
And when he saw that she ate of the fruit
He was excited she fell to a lie.

Now Death would never forget that day
When his vaunted desire would have its sway
Upon mankind and every type of life
For now he would butcher, destroy and slay.

Death entered the world through the gate of sin,
All creatures were affected and hemmed in;
It was God'd judgment upon faithless man
Where no one could ever escape or win.

And thus Death reigned supreme with utmost glee
While billions of men attempted to flee
From its horrid hand, asking agent Fear
If respite be had, but Fear heard no plea.

Death in turn feared when Elijah restored
Life to the widow's son whom she adored
Until he flexed his muscles and attacked
The life restored: it was life he abhorred,

The young maid, and the widow's son at Nain
And Lazarus all came to life again
When Jesus spoke a word and said, arise
Come forth, but they died when their health did wane.

When Jesus surrendered to death a while
Death jumped for joy for his malice and guile,
But he and Satan trembled with great fear
When Jesus rose, and they fell down servile.

The Lord was first to rise from the dead
And to die no more, the saints' living head
And when He comes again, they too will rise
From death's corruption to true life instead.

Death has his sport and will punch his blows
Until the time arrives when no one knows
When he, with Hell and Satan will be cast
Into the lake of fire of utmost woes.

THE TREE

I will speak of what multitudes know
Of a tree which flourished long ago
Before the making of paper was known
Or fields were mechanically sown.

From seedling to a giant it grew
Adorned by green leaves of every hue,
While pregnant branches carried hard fruit
Nourished by the water seeking root.

When clouds vanished and heaven was blue,
Its leaves collected the drops of dew;
The weary farmer rested his head
Beneath its shade on the earth, his bed.

Did Jesus once lean against that tree?
Against its strong arm, His cross to be?
And shelter from the heat of the sun
Before His earthly journey had run?

Land birds perched on its arms to rest,
Prepared for their new fledglings a nest,
While at its fallen decaying leaves
Men could observe how the spider weaves.

No boat was built of its wood, no ship
To float on the sea and roll and dip;
No house or palace or wooden shed
Possessed from its skeleton a bed.

But from its branches, fallen and torn,
The amber flame was often reborn
Where men slumbered and let their minds stray
To muse on the events of the day.

One morning the tree fell to the axe,
It was transported upon mules' backs,
Was nailed to another, freed from moss,
To build a lonely reclining cross.

Upon its limbs, now barren and dry
The Son of God was to bleed and die;
Man cuts the tree in mountain and plain
To hang his fellow to die in pain.

Christ wrought with chisel, hammer and plane
Excellent works, respecting the grain;
Nazareth's carpenter matched the wood
Till articles of perfection stood.

Sometimes I ask did He ever place
One beam across another's face
Then ponder upon the solemn price
He was to offer, the Sacrifice?

Symbol of increase, of fruition,
Of slow torture in man's tradition,
Symbol of death and damnation
Is symbol of lie and salvation.

WHEN JESUS DIED

"The veil of the temple was rent in twain...the earth did quake...and the graves were opened..." (Matthew 27:51, 52).

When Jesus died the Earth strained at its mooring,
Creation reeled as if it quit enduring,
The land convulsed and by shaking had spoken
That Earth's frame bent when its Maker was broken.

Well might the stars have left their lofty stations
And galaxies fell from their sure foundations,
The universe burnt, bursting and colliding
Had not the Father kept all things abiding.

The angels gazed, bewildered, crowding, swooping:
Their Creator died, His holy head drooping,
The sun wore black, the world's Light was extinguished,
A lonely man, but totally distinguished.

But just before, all Heaven quaked and trembled,
Angels were startled where they all assembled,
His shout pierced the skies while the pillars of Hell
Moved and swayed and cracked as they crumbled and fell.

When Jesus died the devil laughed and bleated
Thinking that God was finally defeated,
Saints left their graves, a wonder signifying
That Christ's death brought life to the dead and dying.

Now God receives men under condemnation
Whom justice claimed for unceasing damnation,
The way to Him was opened and made certain
When celestial hands tore the Temple's curtain.

Raised by the Spirit, the Lord then ascended
To Heaven in view of men he defended,
Death's ravage by Life was part of His story
Which He will complete when He comes in glory.

LONELINESS

"Then all the disciples forsook him, and fled (Matthew 26:56).

Jesus struggled when facing the great flood
Of sin and death, and sweated drops of blood:
His friends left Him to pray alone to God
While they slept, while they slept.

He was arrested as the torches blazed
While his disciples stood dumbfounded, dazed:
For just a moment they pondered amazed
Then they fled, then they fled.

The lonely Lamb then faced a vicious pack
When injustice and envy showed no lack
Of violence as soldiers rent His back
With a whip, with a whip.

He bore it in silence, no tears were shed
Though the stripes were fierce and His body bled;
They spat upon His face and crowned His head
With the thorns, with the thorns.

No one was present who could understand
From the raging crowd or the soldiers' band
Why Jesus gave Himself, stretching each hand
For the nails, for the nails.

All this was nothing to truly compare
With His deep torment which no man could share
That God, His Father, could not look or stare
At His Son, at His Son.

Each of us wondered, like a sheep has strayed,
Each ruffled his bed of sin where he laid,
Yet for these sins the awful debt was paid
With His blood, with His blood.

CONDESCENSION

"And the Word was made flesh and dwelt among us"
(John 1:14).

And were you born like other sons of men
With blood and water on you crinkled skin?
And was the sound of praise to God heard when
You breathed and cried in the cave of the inn?
And did you suckle on your mother's breast
And crawl upon your little hands and knees?
Great God who spread the sky from east to west,
Whom angels praised and delighted to please.

And did your mother hold you by the hand
And teach you how to walk and dress and speak?
And did you fall, not knowing how to stand,
Who made man's feet to sprint, his tongue unique?
And did you preach to men the word of life,
Calling them to repent and turn to God
While they despised you, urging you to strife
And said that you served in the devil's squad.

And did you see the soldiers passing by
With slaves in chains, ill clad, wounded, sore?
Till they were raised upon crosses to die
Ravaged by pain, bearing their sweat and gore?
You saw and knew that this will be the lot
Which you must endure to do your Father's will,
That you would bear man's sin and every blot
By tasting death upon that lonely hill.

And did they lay you on a slab of stone
And wrap you tightly with a linen cloth?
Until you rose from the dark grave alone
And showed that God has turned away his wrath?
The mystery of mysteries must be
The Shepherd died to gather His sheep in
That Christ the Lord was born a man for me
And gave His life for the vile creature's sin.

DISHONOURED

Dishonoured was He beyond degree
And then was nailed to the wood of the tree;
Two thieves were His companions to be
When Jesus suffered on Calvary.

What really happened on Calvary?
Upon that middle cross of three?
The Lord of life, for you and for me
Surrendered His life to set us free.

He lifted our burden: we must flee
To the Saviour upon bended knee;
The day is coming when I shall see
The scars of His wounds that bled for me.

THE CRUCIFIED

"And when they were come to the place, which is called Calvary, there they crucified him" (Luke 23:33).

It was in the garden of Gethsemane
Where Christ the Saviour sorely wept
As His disciples slept;
Where men, like thieves, upon Him crept;
There, He knelt and fervently prayed
Until the hour He was betrayed
For thirty silver pieces, paid
By men who judged they could afford
To pay for Him a mean reward.

The moon had hid away its light,
The sun removed its robes of white,
Crickets broke the silence of night
As he struggled away from sight
In the garden of agony,
Where His sweat drops, like rubies fell
To speak of His sorrow so well
Of whom the Scriptures did foretell
He will break the power of Hell
By His deep pain and agony.

The crimson from His brow did flow
Through torment only He could know.
Many a man would die with pride,
Despise the gallows and deride

While heartless men will gloat and chide.
Bruised by whips of animal hide,
His feet stumbled, he could not stride
As He carried His cross and tried
To keep it on His back and side
While Satan's host hurried to ride
To see that Christ was crucified.

His anguished heart was free from fear
That hardened men would sneer and jeer
Or that His blood will smear His skin,
But that His soul will bear man's sin
When guilt was laid on Him that day
So that His Father looked away.

Who knew pain as the Crucified?
Who felt His soul putrefied?
Not even the thieves mortified
Who for their deeds of guilt had died.
He rent the Heavens when he cried:
Water and blood flowed from His side.

On Calvary's cross of dire shame,
Life is dead, the light-footed lame,
Victims are deemed sport for the game;
None could boast his pedigree or name.
Men, with fervour, mock the dying,
Laughter, mirth and jokes supplying
With raised voices, God defying;
No pity when a body fails,
Hands feeling the bite of the nails.
What mind can ever try to sound
God's wisdom on Calvary's mound?
The hill, the battlefield for man
Where Hell's demons to battle ran

And were defeated in their plan
And man is saved by Christ the Man.

The Lord of life, creation's head
Gave his life for the living dead:
A sacrifice of awesome dread.
Of His pleasure He came to save
Men whom evil did once enslave
In the darkest dungeon and cave.

Their risen bodies will yet fly
To their great Redeemer on high
When this Earth turns to fiery red,
When graves throw out their silent dead,
When the Lamb is the judge instead.
Christ rose triumphant from the dead,
He did leave His burial bed
The bed of stone on which He stayed
When His shrouded body was laid
Until He crushed the Devil's head.

Who would think that on a dry tree
God would release the sinner free?
It is the greatest mystery.
Once He determined to save man
He set to accomplish His plan
To pardon sin and save the soul,
Make ransomed men and women whole;
They are His treasure and His prize,
His home is theirs beyond the skies.

SALVATION

"The Son of God was manifested, that he might destroy the works of the devil" (1John 3:8).

With heavy chains he drowned in sin
And did not seek a chink of light;
Rebellious pride settled within
His blighted soul, slave of the night.

Lost was the day of pure delight
Which was his at the dawn of time
When man was holy in God's sight
Before Adam acted his crime.

Deep in the cave of sin he lay,
No hope to cheer a spirit bound
Until the Saviour won the day
And lifted his soul from the ground.

The time was ripe for the great fight:
God, clothed in flesh stood on the Earth,
Wielded His righteousness and might
And freed the sinner by new birth,

The battle for the soul of man
Was fought by man, yet God the same
And though the foe took flight and ran
Yet he was crushed before His name.

Glorious the Lord for sinners slain
For in His blood is life and balm;
Satan can never rise again:
Is chained forever by the Lamb.

Sing forth the song of victory:
The Christ has won the life of men;
Great is the God of mystery,
The God of sea, and hill, and fen.

SACRIFICE

The passing of the days, the years,
Promises renewed, wasted tears
Cannot blot the guilt away;
The soul must have the cure it needs
To heal the wounds of sinful deeds:
A blood that was shed one day,

How can it be that blood will heal
Bruises which my heart does feel
And ill from its sinews grown?
The blood is of the Holy One
Who came to save us when undone
Who trod the winepress alone.

The stain of sin He will remove
And to my guilty conscience prove
That He is willing and can.
My soul will die if not redeemed
By blood which on Golgotha streamed
To rescue a dying man.

CHRIST CONQUERD

He stared at death with flint-like courage
Submitting to unmeasured shame,
While men flocked from city and village
Eager to murder and defame.

Shouting as in the day of pillage,
Howling like blood hounds for the game,
They gave their King for Rome to savage
Though Pilate found in Him no blame.

The blackness of hell marred His visage
When sin was laid upon His frame
For Jesus the Lord paid His homage
To death for those He chose to claim.

He suffered with the certain knowledge
That death will flee before His name;
Hell and Satan could not envisage
Their servile action in His aim.

Death was killed and in the ravage
Satan lay bound, helpless and lame;
All people shout out loud the message
The Christ conquered and overcame.

BEARER OF MY SIN

"Behold the Lamb of God, which taketh away the sin of the world" (John 1:29).

Bearer of my sin that day,
You rested in the tomb in sleep;
On the third day You broke away
Saved me from damnation's scrapheap.

Gone is the guilt that once was mine;
I stand righteous before the throne;
Your blood flowed like the deepest wine,
Lord Jesus, who came to atone.

Now filled with love for love divine,
My eyes will weep, my heart will sigh;
My Saviour, head of the new line,
Let me be Yours, to live and die.

Thus bought by blood I rest my soul
On Christ and bid Him rule my ways,
His service shall be my one goal
Throughout the remnant of my days.

FOR ME

"The Son of God, who loved me and gave himself for me"
(Galatians 2:20).

For me, for me You came to die
So many years before my birth;
The anguish of Your dying cry
Pierced through the heavens and the earth.

Your skin was torn, Your body bled,
The nails transfixed You on the tree;
God's vengeance fell upon Your head
As You suffered and died for me.

Great darkness fell upon the land:
Transaction between God and Man
Was certified by God's own hand,
Salvation wrought for sinful man.

But yet the Lord was pleased to slay:
His holy wrath was satisfied;
You paid my ransom on that day:
The way to God was opened wide.

Your friends escaped, Your mother wept,
You faced hell's agony alone
Before You tasted death and slept
And rested on a slab of stone.

The chain of death could not hold fast
The Prince of life, the meek, the brave:
God's Spirit, true from first to last
Raised up the Christ from the dark grave.

Praise be to God, the One in Three,
The wisdom, sacrifice, the might;
To You shall my obedience be
Till faith is transformed into sight.

O SWORD OF GOD

O Sword of God cleaving asunder,
Piercing of bone the marrow,
We fall before You and surrender
As clods before the harrow.

O Word of God, loud roaring thunder,
Look on this vale of sorrow;
We hear Your voice with awe and wonder,
Give life to a dry furrow.

Spirit of God, let us not squander
Our life, today, tomorrow,
Bring us to Christ each time we wander
In paths both broad and narrow.

CONSECRATION

Be my fortress, be my shield
In this world of sin and woe,
To Your will my will I yield,
In Your shadow I will grow.
O my Lord, I was a stranger
Living in the depth of night;
You have saved my soul from danger,
Lead me in the path of light.

Let me see Jesus before me
Dying for my sins so great;
Holy, pure and faultless was He,
Plucked me from a hell-bound fate,
Fill my poor heart with Your Spirit:
I will increase in Your love;
I will call men to inherit
Eternal life with You above.

Living Saviour, it was Your blood
That dripped upon the soil in death:
O my eyes, burst into a flood,
Sing my voice with all your breath.
Nought is health and life without You,
Like the dry dust of the field;
True commitment I now renew,
Fruit abundant I will yield.

A PLEA

Great Lord of glory and of might
Of majesty beyond degree;
Effulgence of unfathomed light,
Unbounded, eternal and free,
Look on me, a child of the night
Ruled by darkness, I cannot see.

God of this wondrous creation,
Of the earth and heaven and sea;
Each star in its constellation
By Your commandment came to be;
Mortal I, son of damnation,
Can You, in mercy, think of me?

The gospel siren once sounded
Reproving me of sin and shame
Till my sad soul was surrounded
By a voice that shouted my name:
Look to Me, my wounds abounded,
Come to Me, for to you I came.

How can it be that He should care
For such a vile sinner as I?
How can it be that He should dare
To humble Himself and to die?
Turn my soul and upon Him stare
And for His boundless mercy cry.

Sleep not my eyes, my aching heart
Till you know you are forgiven
Until your shackles fall apart
And you feel the joy of heaven;
Calvary alone forms the start
Of new life when grace is given.

THE RED CARD

"In whom we have redemption through his blood, the forgiveness of sin, according to the riches of his grace" (Ephesians 1:7).

Sir, I heard your friend prophesy
That on the day that you will die
You will enter paradise,
The blessed home of the wise;
Do you possess a Green Card?
Did you earn it? Was it hard?

Not so, my dear, my card is red,
A precious free gift to me, I said.
Why a red colour? She cried,
Did you have it painted, dyed?
No, dipped in blood, I replied,
The blood of God's Lamb who died.

BLIND BARTIMEUS

"And Jesus stood still, and commanded him to be called"
(Mark 10:49).

Timeus' son sat on the street
To beg for alms of coin and meat,
To plead for handouts, ask for bread
While flies explored his face and head.

He begged when he lost his eyesight
And missed the guidance of the light;
He could do nothing else but cry
And seek pity from passers-by.

The Saviour passed, there was a sound
As rushing crowds gathered around,
The blind man saw his chance at hand
And shouted like a roaring band.

The crowd told him to shut his mouth
And not be like a blabbermouth,
But Jesus heard his shout for help,
The shout of agony, a yelp.

"David's son, have mercy on me";
The Lord stood still, He heard his plea:
Bring him to me was his reply:
No entreaty from Him must die

"He calls for you", the people said,
"A guiding hand leads you ahead",
The man threw all hindrance away
With frenzied zeal to find his way.

"I need no riches, please be kind,
Pity me Lord, for I am blind,
Restore the sight of my dark eyes
That I may see green earth, blue skies".

The tender Lord was never slow
To pity one whose tears did flow;
The blindness vanished with a word,
The sound of praise could then be heard.

O Lord, the weight of sin makes blind
The heart of man, his will and mind;
Send out Your word to give new sight
To those who live in darkest night.

THE BLIND CHILD
(Based on an anonymous Arabic poem).

Mother, what shape is the sky?
What is the moon or the light?
You speak of their splendour
Which is obscured from my sight;
Is the world filled with darkness
Like the blackness I see?
My mother, give me your hand
And do not go far from me.

I walk, but fear to stumble,
Alike the night as the day
With no guidance for my steps
Whether short or long the way;
I wonder, on my pathway,
Which may be rugged or plain
If I should meet with danger
And holes to trap me again.

My stick remains my eyesight,
But does it see with an eye?
Does it breathe, suffer and feel?
Does it listen when I cry?
The children play around me
Not knowing worry or fear
While I am blind and lonely
With their shouting in my ear;

It is God who observes me,
Keeps my steps lest I fall,
Shows me kindness in my life
When for his mercy I call.

ALFRED

He was my brother in the Lord
Who felt Hitler's unholy sword.
He said, bury me when I die,
Let not the sparks lick me and fry,
But place me deep within the ground.
Burn me not with a sizzling sound,
The sad fate of my family
Which felt the burning bodily
 As sinews melted from the bone
In the furnace where they were thrown.
Mother, you faced them without hope
When they transformed your fat to soap.
Have they not seen you purified
Their stinking flesh, though putrefied?
There is no hell the foolish say,
Hell sees their deeds and runs away.

I was born a Bavarian Jew,
But who could tell that we would rue
That we belonged to such a land
Where human devils were to stand?
They baked us in the heated fire
As building bricks for their empire.
Can I forget them as they dragged
My mother as they laughed and bragged?
But pastor Frank saved me from hell
When at Christ's feet I humbly fell.
I know I shall never return
To where we were hunted and spurned.

Now I am old, ready to die,
To see my Saviour in the sky;
Cremation was my kindred's fate,
Let me enter death's earthen gate,
Let my body be interred,
But let me not be scorched and burned.

WHEN TIME TRAMPLED ON HER HEAD

Beyond the city alleys
Where golden food crops grow,
Within the glens and valleys
Where waters edge and flow,
She picked the blood red poppies
The slender drops of snow.

I answer if you ask me:
"Has beauty's crown been won?"
'Look not to the apple tree
Which blossoms in the sun:
Beauty, dressed in flesh, could see,
Could talk and leap and run.'

Like jasmine of the orient
She filled the heart with glee:
Nimble, youthful and salient,
Bright, vivacious, free;
Her face was far more radiant
Than sun beams on the sea.

When time trampled on her head
It plucked its hair quite thin;
Eyes turned dim and ears like lead
With bristles on her chin;
Her face, like a ruffled bed,
Showed sunspots on the skin.

Age worked hard its cold steel mill
And crumpled her pure brow;
With its creeping perfect skill
It caused her back to bow;
In her features one sees still
Signs of past beauty, now.

She waits for death to vanquish
Her body in its hold;
Her legs, once pretty, languish
Beneath her weight and fold;
Heaven will have no anguish
But streets of light and gold.

LIFE

"It is appointed unto men once to die, but after this the judgment" (Hebrews 9:27).

The echo of a wailing voice, returned by the hills,
Answers the agony of soul when death strikes and kills.
Until the mind cannot forget its torment and ills.

Fountains emerging from red eyes gushed upon the ground
Like sorely weeping summer skies where monsoons abound,
Will the merciless hand of time heal a wound unbound?

Will salty waters from sad eyes join rivers that flow
Across the plains and rocky land, reeling as they go?
Or will the longing of the heart ride the sea of woe?

The proud mother enjoys her child for a little while,
Then sprinkles soil on his box when life proceeds with guile,
His face is gone, his shout, his call, his laugh, play and smile.

The bride, wondrous in appearance on her wedding day,
Wails upon her husband's corpse, soon to join the clay,
None can procure balm or hope when death collects its pay.

Children bury their own parents, feeling biting grief,
The earth has taken to stealing, has become a thief;
Corruption turns beauty to dust while man's life is brief.

Human life is a worthless game if for aye we die
And is the greatest mockery underneath the sky
If we should perish forever with a final sigh.

If man's spirit does not endure when his days have run,
How hopeless then his destiny since time had begun:
The dead soared to eternity, to meet God each one.

THE REAPER

"Death passed upon all men" (Romans 5:12).

Pass O Reaper, pass me by,
See I am no longer fresh,
Fat and flabby is my flesh,
Hard my hearing, dim my eye.
Pass O Reaper, pass me by.

I shall pass, but will return
When your flabby flesh will rot
Like a rump broiled in the pot;
Better if your dust will turn
Into ashes when you burn.

Sharpen blade when you come back,
Let the cut be swift and clean,
Be the craftsman when you glean;
I do not think that you lack
Practice when you strike and hack.

Give me sleep, let me not see
Your sharpened steel gleaming bright
As it cuts me from the light;
Take my body, set me free
While true life beckons to me.

NOT TONIGHT

Leaving the womb, a moonless night,
We take a breath and cry with might,
Howling as we first meet the light
As battling men with death in sight.

We flourish and increase in height,
Life throbs in veins, the world is bright,
Our souls forbid evil to blight
The will to live, however slight.

The sunset years precede the night
Age comes with pain to wound and bite,
As death draws near we cry with fright:
Not yet, not yet, no, not tonight.

THE FALLOF BABYLON-536 B.C.

"He consulted with images, he looked in the liver"
(Ezekiel 21:21).

The catapults fly while valiant men try
To redress the damage;
The feared end is nigh, the old women sigh,
Dogs gather to scavenge.

Sturdy mothers cry as their husbands die
In the war most savage;
The virgin, too shy, must make bare her thigh,
Ready for the ravage.

The tide has turned, the city is burned
With none to deliver;
Surrender is spurned while death returned
To empty its quiver.

Our strong bowels churned when the sword was earned,
We looked in the liver,
But we sadly learned that our gods have yearned
That blood forms a river.

JUDGMENT

When He cried, the heavens were rent
Until in death His head was bent,
Lord Jesus, by the Father sent,
Who made our flesh His home, His tent,
The tent which for a while He left
When on the cross He died bereft
Beside two men condemned for theft.

The heavens will be rent again
When Jesus comes back with His train,
Upon all men to rule and reign
When the final trumpet shall sound
And all men rise up from the ground.

Upon the clouds He shall descend;
The earthling's days shall not extend
When life upon this earth shall end;
When men at last tremble to meet
The Judge while falling at His feet.
They shall see Him upon the throne,
Their guarded secrets shall be known
As guilty hearts confess their own
While bodies, in corruption sown,
Shall the incorruptible wear
But those whom corruption did snare

Will cry with deep remorse and wail
While ransomed men shall praise and hail
With pure hearts and exultant cords
The King of kings and Lord of lords.

What wondrous day that day shall be
When every eye the Christ shall see
The One who died upon the tree;
Then will heaven and earth subside
And no man can escape or hide.
The wicked shall know and perceive
That it is too late to retrieve
Their evil deeds against mankind
Wrought in the name of humankind.
All men shall see Him and declare;
His lordship and upon Him stare;
Those who denied His nature twain
Shall tremble in the Lamb's domain.

Will you not hear the Gospel's call
Before judgment comes to enthral
The sinners who will not repent
Whose mind upon evil is bent?

HELL

"Where their worm dieth not, and the fire is not quenched"
(Mark 9:48).

A place of horror, fearful awe,
Deep agony and thoughts that gnaw
Upon the soul in painful ways
With no escape for evermore.

Regret, regret of what was missed,
The glory of those that Heaven kissed:
Exchanged for wretchedness and woe,
For flames that will not be dismissed.

If only, if once, I took heed
To listen to them who did plead
That I see what is clear and plain
And to repent with utmost speed.

The gnawing thoughts, the deep regret,
The folly, I cannot forget,
The loss I had will ever be
Like worms that gnaw at a courgette.

Should I burn for a billion years?
I then would know an end to tears,
But to regret for evermore
Is awful, in the flame that sears.

INJUSTICE

Say, Injustice, when were you born?
When did your eyes first see the morn?
You seem each day to be reborn

Since your first parents went astray,
Since they departed from God's way
I am reborn anew each day.

Tell, Injustice, where do you live?
You seem all creatures to outlive:
Bloodshed and theft are gifts you give.

I live where man chooses to be,
I read his open heart and see
That sin makes him no longer free.

What are the deeds you like to do
Which none seems able to undo,
When men receive wages from you?

I place the just behind barbed wire,
Do the wicked man's desire,
Consume the poor with flames of fire.

Men heed me and slay each other,
They crush human rights and smother,
I set brother against brother.

I cause people to die in pan,
Destroy produce in field and plain,
Close ears to the cry of the slain.

I send the innocent to death,
Rob him of life as if by stealth
And fan his pyre with his own breath.

I beat men, give them their gruel.
Afflict them by means most cruel
Using Freedom's sons for fuel.

No class or kind escapes my hand,
They may face me as one strong band,
Yet on their necks is where I stand.

I catch the unborn in my net
Whose parents refuse to beget:
Would rather play and then forget.

I urge a man to leave his wife,
Rob her of youth then bare his knife,
Count her the mistake of his life.

Injustice, how else are you called?
I remember that I was told
Your name brings terror to the bold.

Oppression is my other name
Through which I earned my vaunted fame
To strike while others take the blame.

Injustice, have you many sons?
Were they nurtured on bread or guns?
The brave flees their fury and runs.

My firstborn twins are my delight:
Their work brings pleasure to my sight
Though they try to regain the right.

They take my weapons and employ
My skills which they learnt to deploy
To hunt the guilty and destroy.

Vengeance, and Hatred, is each name;
Man's torment is their chiefest game
Till he asks not from where it came.

What constitutes your greatest deed
On which your soul must live and feed?
Is it adultery or greed?

My deeds are many, full of lust,
The one I must do, yes I must
Is to accuse and slay the just.

A gambler may lose then regain,
The shackled may sever his chain,
But life once lost, lives not again.

Injustice, begone into hell;
Let Justice flourish and do well;
May you never buy men and sell.

CHRIST WILL REMEMBER

Ponder the experience of man;
Turmoil and pain, struggle and toil,
Faces driven into the soil,
Smudged into the filth and dirt
By greedy men, scourge of the earth,
Self-sufficient lovers of mirth
Until the poor begin to flirt
With death that it may lose its way
And take its hideous face away.

Men, with a mighty boastful hand
Crush the feeble with studied boots
And pluck him from his very roots;
They scatter him across the land
And treat him lesser than the brutes.

Children are born and children die,
Young men grow old, women will try
To hide time's hand with painted face:
Crumbling bones beneath silken lace.
The span of love and joy will last
Till disappointment, like a worm
Nibbles the weak heart and the firm
And men are like refuse outcast.
Though strength will flourish for a while,
It fades as fades and put-on smile.
The years disable all who live
Who try to buy what life can give.

And in the darkness of the tomb,
Black as the blackness of the womb,
The mind is blind to every sight,
Sense organs cannot sense the light,
Ears are deaf to the sound of life:
Thunder of canons, shout of me
While babies cry amidst the strife,
Their bellies like a vacant den,
Crying until time stops their breath.
Then they will fall into the grave
To join the scoundrel and the brave:
They could not tell the day from night,
Nor comprehend crawling and flight,
Yet they will share the fate of man,
Discarded like an empty can.

In such a state, early or late,
Devoid of love, empty of hate,
I ask if faith can see beyond
The fiery lake and limy pond,
Burst to life like leaf and frond
And to eternal life respond?
Will he reject dollar and yen?
And scatter hope to dying men
Before wriggling worm, slimy slug
Creep on the grave with snail and bug?
Will it yet ask when life is dead?
And corruption like cancer spread,
Will Christ the Lord remember us?

We share the throes of earthly woe:
Stinking bodies reduced to bones
Hidden beneath the clay and stones
Where eye sees not or brains dare know
How men break up like melting snow,

Or seething sea that will enmesh
With weeds and worms the rotting flesh,
Then with the passing of the years
Men will forget their wailing tears
That on the open grave once flowed,
For time will send its healing balm
To fill the mind with soothing calm
Like clouds that gather and unload
Their rain upon budding flowers
Where snails wake up in the showers:
Memories fade upon life's road.

Some will remember till they die
Their loved ones who succumbed and went,
Whose numbered days were wholly spent.
The flood of tears may one day dry:
Their voices call, their spirits cry
For those upon whom time has sent
Its gleaming axe till they were bent.
They will recall, yet One remains
Whose effulgent life never wanes:
Jesus the Lord will not forget.
He shall raise our bodies anew,
Fresher than morning air and dew
Of decomposed earthly remains,
Of mouldy lungs and mouldy brains
Which hold the bones, the bloody stains
Of the dead beneath the amber:
Yes indeed, Christ will remember.

THE LAST DAY

"The trumpet shall sound, and the dead shall be raised"
(1 Corinthians 15:52).

Tremble at the last trumpet's call,
Down on your face and begin to crawl,
Are you mighty enough to stand
As you enter the judgment hall?
God comes to sentence and command
All the rich and poor of the land.
Approach, all men, the great and small,
Release your dead ye desert sand,
The Day of Judgment is at hand.
Its sight and sound will make you fall.

Cast out your dead, ye raging seas:
Return the souls you felled like trees,
Have you not heard trumpets calling?
All life within you will now cease.
Have you not seen mountains falling?
The sight of the end appalling?
Roll your white billows as you please,
Stop, ye ships, begone your trawling,
Time has ended, no time for brawling,
Ye deed, kneel down upon your knees.

Ashes born in the flames of fire,
Restore your dead men from the mire,
Ashes scattered into the air,
Remake the old and worn out sire,
Form the visage of young and fair
In Indus valley and city square.
Valiant men, builders of empire,
Will your unbending steel hearts dare
Into God's holiness to stare
Having kindled many a pyre?

Turn your eyes, you cannot look:
Your heart is as the blackest rook,
Your evil deeds will be outspread
When God will open Heaven's book.
The sins that were your drink and bread
Are part of you, on them you fed,
Your spite flowed as a winter's brook,
Lament aloud, hang down your head,
Utter darkness shall be your bed
With those who said: God will not look.

Rise up and flee! The hour has come!
Drown yourself in gin and rum.
Will you shelter beneath the ground?
You will see of your deeds the sum.
Close your ears to the painful sound,
Rising as the squeal of the hound:
The wailing cry, the moaning hum

Of men whose glory was earthbound,
Whose boastful words did once resound,
Reared in palace and reared in slum.

Earth will burn with a great burning,
Ended are research and learning,
The world, by evil polluted,
Will halt its spinning and its turning.
It will be plucked out, uprooted
Till its shameful cry is muted.
Heaven with its new adorning
Of just men, prepared and suited,
Whose life in their God was rooted
Will glory in a new morning.

Lord, I fear for men and women
Who will not partake of Heaven.
While I bless You for salvation,
I wish they could be forgiven.
Men from every tribe and nation
Have escaped the condemnation.
I quake at the sentence given
On those marked for damnation
With no hope of restoration
When into Hell they are driven.

Almighty God, send down Your grace
On the lost of the human race.

MORNING PRAYER

For rest in sleep throughout the night,
The hand which held us with its might,
For singing birds that greet the light
We praise Your name, Heavenly Father.

That the pain subsided as we slept,
That comfort reached us as it crept,
For mercy which healed us and kept,
We give You thanks, Heavenly Father.

Give us courage to face the day,
Show us the pitfalls in our way,
Guide us in all we do and say,
That we may honour You, Heavenly Father.

For those with a broken spirit,
Subdued, failing to inherit
Solace in Christ and His merit,
We pray for heavenly joy, Father.

Some find this life a heavy load,
Hunger and sickness pierce and goad,
Send them sustenance on their road

And rest in You, Heavenly Father.

The widow, the orphan the poor,
Whose troubles seem to have no cure,
The oppressed who cannot endure,
We pray for them Heavenly Father.

Your children on the sea and land,
All my loved ones fed by Your hand,
Be their support that they may stand
In life and death in Christ, O Father.

Let all men praise You and extol,
We gladly surrender our all;
Let us see the gates of Hell fall
Before Your Christ, Heavenly Father.

EVENING PRAYER

O Lord, the night draws to enclose
Our souls, ready for repose,
As now in sleep our eyelids close,
Watch over us Heavenly Father.

Almighty, whose eyes never sleep,
Guard my loved ones as shadows creep,
Comfort the sad who mourn and weep,
Heal their wounds, Heavenly Father.

Look down upon us through the night,
Let no nightmare or ill affright,
Let our thoughts be holy and right,
Give us dreams of Heaven, O Father.

Support the poor, restore the weak,
Uphold the pure, sustain the meek,
When we are lost, let us all seek
The way that leads to You, O Father.

Be with the men upon the seas,
Refresh them with the gentle breeze,
Let all danger banish and cease,
Come to their aid, Heavenly Father.

Remember those who soon will die,
Let them in their sickness rely
Upon Your mercy to supply
Eternal peace, Heavenly Father.

Think of the bereaved, lonely, old,
Be to them more precious than gold,
Make their spirits steadfast and bold:
They have no other help, O Father.

Forgive the sins of this past day,
The unkind word that we did say;
Humble our hearts in every way
To live for You, Heavenly Father.

Grant our bodies a quiet rest,
Let us be numbered with the blest,
Be strong on our behalf to rest
Our souls from outer darkness, Father.

Should You call our spirits to be
In Your presence, happy and free,
We cry aloud on bended knee,
Uphold those who remain, O Father.

www.ingramcontent.com/pod-product-compliance
Lightning Source LLC
Chambersburg PA
CBHW071620080526
44588CB00010B/1203